C.P.R. For Women

A Woman's Guide to Resuscitating Her Life

Learn how to (c)hoose wisely, (p)repare your mind and (r)eact to life's challenges

Laura Lawson

C.P.R. For Women

A Woman's Guide to Resuscitating Her Life

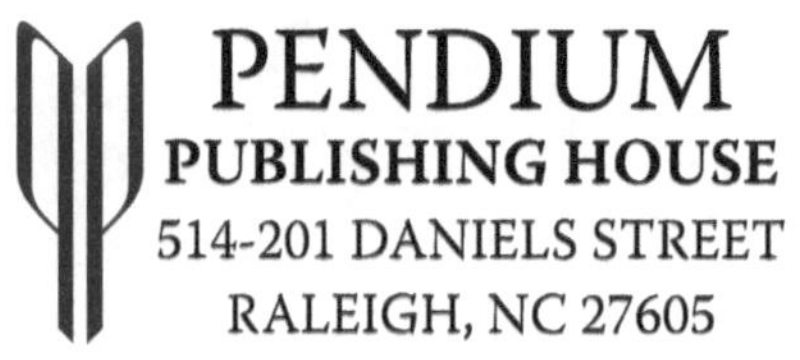

PENDIUM
PUBLISHING HOUSE
514-201 DANIELS STREET
RALEIGH, NC 27605

For information, please visit our Web site at
www.pendiumpublishing.com

PENDIUM Publishing and its logo
are registered trademarks.

C.P.R. for Women
A Woman's Guide to Resuscitating Her Life
By Laura Lawson

Copyright © Laura Lawson, 2012
All Rights Reserved.

ISBN: 978-1-936513-34-5

PUBLISHER'S NOTE

This book is printed on acid-free paper.

Table of Contents

Favorite Quote

When one door closes another opens. But often we look so long, so regretfully upon the closed door that we fail to see the one that has opened for us.

Helen Keller

(C.P.R) for Women
Introduction

This book will help reshape the way you live, work, manage money, and deal with intimate relationships with your family, friends, lovers and most important God. Have you ever found yourself all revved up to start something new, but then losing steam and interest too quickly? You now feel tired, burnt out and emotionally dead inside. You need (C.P.R); a woman's guide to resuscitating her life. You often feel this emotional emptiness because you have not learned to focus on unfinished business and deal with all the things in your life needing healing, closure, and surrender.

Your current situation is marking a period of deep emotional awareness. You might need to dive deep into your soul at a discomforting level. Look at the choices you have made and take a good look at YOUR role in your life, career, financial and relationship problems. It can be a time of "chickens coming home to roost" anywhere in your life where you have refused to take responsibility. This is now an opportunity, even though it may feel like a curse. Learn how to **C**hoose wisely, **P**repare your mind and **R**eact to challenges in your life.

Love and Romance

Maybe something has happened and this is a tough time in your relationship when you or your partner may need to lean on each other more often than ever before. Couples often get stuck in routines and patterns which foster codependency issues. This can create a "come here, now go away" effect when you want your partner to open up. Then you get all skittish about his or her "neediness" once that happens. Try to keep fireworks in the bedroom because you are liable to pick fights when you are trying to resolve your inner conflict. REMEMBER that this is YOUR issue, and it is not your mate's job to absorb your frustration.

Sometimes your own confidence may be the culprit of any relationship speed bumps based on feelings of self-worth and shakiness about yourself. Get clear about your values. Do you and your mate want the same things? Where your goals do not align, is it necessarily a deal breaker? Take time to think about what YOU want and separate from anything else in your life.

Understand there is a difference between marriage and dating. In terms of marriage, make sure your mate is faithful to God first then they will always be faithful to you. When you are yoked up to the one you are supposed to be with, you will have fulfillment. God did not say that it would be easy. All that dating stuff was a facade. I believe that when you date you never meet the real person, you meet their secretary. The secretary intercepts or filters and only allows things that are considered positive or beneficial to the cause to be presented. The cause is clearly to win the interest and affection of that person you seek. When you finally meet the real person, you may find that you do not really like their personality and you may want out of the relationship. Unfortunately some of us do not have any staying power. Take time to learn and know the real person. In most relationships, it is not until you and your partner reach the five to eight year mark that you may experience or notice severe drama or craziness. Most people want to abort the mission only to have to start all over again with the same drama in a new relationship. You end up with a new relationship but same drama.

Stop living in a selfish mindset because it should not be about you but about others and something greater. Keep on giving everything in that relationship as long as you are grounded in God's word. Even when it seems that you are the only one giving, keep on trying because your conversation will win them over. Do not abort the relationship by getting out and acting like it never happened. You will end up starting the cycle all over again. Someone has to have and needs staying power. Remember that what you respect, you will not hurt and will attract respect in return. What you disrespect will move away from you. Eventually because of hurt, nobody is respecting anybody.

In terms of dating do not be unequally yoked in your romantic relationships. Women need to learn to wait, be patient and fall back. Let the man find you. "He that findeth a wife findeth a good thing" Proverbs 18:22. Sometimes you will think that you are ready for something and God will carry you through situations to prove to you that you are not ready. Just wait on Him and though it tarries believe it will come. A relationship that God does not ordain will draw you further from God and a relationship that is ordained will draw you closer to God.

Learn to let go of some things and some people who are not going in the same direction. Learn to lay aside things to be able to grasp what God has planned for you. Sometimes He will challenge you to let go of something so that He can give you something else. Be multidimensional and know that although you are living in this moment your mind should be operating in your future. When you let go of something negative know that you cannot go back. When feeling lonely, remember the source of your hurt, stress and pain. Let your past be your past and walk into your future. Change the way you think tonight and you will start getting different results.

You have to realize where you are contributing to the problems in your life. Take ownership of your issues. If you are able to do this you will experience a complete turnaround in your love life. In this book I have listed some "food for thought". With the help of my closest friends and family, who have all experienced hurt and pain of some kind in their lives, I have listed thirty one ways to resuscitate your mind, body, spirit and intimate relationships. Here is your daily bread for one month. Begin each day by meditating on ways to have a more satisfying love life. Share this with other ladies. You will make someone SMILE, another RETHINK her choices and another woman PREPARE. We have all heard these rules before but no one has ever told us why we should follow them. I am always asking why and through life experiences and talking to various women in my personal circle I got answers.

Thirty-One Days to Resuscitate your Love Life

Day 1. **If a man wants you, nothing can keep him away.**
Why? I have found that love is a two-way street. You have to constantly evaluate your relationship. A good yardstick for how one treats (and is treated by) their significant other is to remember that love is patient, love is kind. It does not envy, it does not boast, it is not proud. It is not rude, it is not self-seeking, it is not easily angered, and it keeps no record of wrongs. Love does not delight in evil but rejoices with the truth. It always protects, always trusts, always hopes, and always perseveres.

Day 2. **If he does not want you, nothing can make him stay.**
Why? Be the woman a man needs, not the woman that needs a man. If he leaves or gives up on you, remember, it is his loss.

Day 3. **Stop making excuses for a man and his behavior.**
Why? I got so accustomed to more bad things happening in a relationship rather than good things until eventually I started to expect the negative things. So often we see more negatives than positives and it is easier to recognize negatives because of what we are typically exposed to. It is sad that we do not recognize a good man because we are so used to the bad ones. So if you need clarity like me, think of love in this way. Love is not impatient or irritable, love is not cruel. It praises positive things about others (their accomplishments, qualities, and good fortune), it does not seek to make others

feel small, and it is humble. It is considerate of your feelings, is concerned about your well-being and happiness, becomes angry only as a last resort, and will always think the best of you.

Day 4. **Allow your INTUITION (or spirit) to save you from heartache.**
Why? It is better to know and be disappointed than to never know and always wonder. No man is worth your tears, and the one who loves you will not make you cry.

Day 5. **Stop trying to change yourselves for a relationship that is not meant to be.**
Why? It is better to be hated for who you are than be loved for someone you are not. Beauty may get the attention but personality gets the heart.

Day 6. **Slower is better.**
Why? A guy does not ever have to be more than a friend, sometimes things are better that way.

Day 7. **NEVER live your life for a man before you find what makes you truly happy.**
Why? Beauty is about living your life and being happy with yourself inside and out. A man willing to do anything just to place a smile on your face is one worth keeping. Be happy.

Day 8. **If a relationship ends because the man was not treating you as you deserve then no, you can't "be friends." A friend would not mistreat a friend.**

Why? It is better to be alone and dignified than to have companionship and be taken advantage of by someone.

Day 9. **Do not settle. If you feel like he is stringing you along then he probably is.**
Why? A wise girl kisses but does not love, listens but does not believe and leaves before she is left.

Day 10. **Do not stay because you think "it will get better." You will be mad at yourself a year later for staying when things are not better.**
Why? If you are not worth the trouble then he is not the worth the time.

Day 11. **The only person you can CONTROL in a relationship is you.**
Why? Remember; if he wants to, he will.

Day 12. **Avoid men who have a bunch of children by a bunch of different women. He did not marry them when he got them pregnant so why would he treat you any differently?**
Why? Just because someone invites you to drama does not mean you have to RSVP.

Day 13. **Always have your OWN set of friends separate from his.**
Why? If you expect him to give you girl time, expect to give him guy time.

Day 14. **Maintain boundaries in how a guy treats you.**

Why? Never let a man hit you and ladies should never hit a man either. Violence is not classy. Respect from others comes from self-respect. Yelling during an argument means you have already lost the fight.

Day 15. If something bothers you, speak up.
Why? You should not need to raise your voice. If you are dealing with a person who will not listen unless you speak forcefully, then they are not worth dealing with. When you need to talk never underestimate the power of warm greeting and a kiss.

Day 16. Never let a man know everything about you if you know nothing about him.
Why? Maintain your mystery; men love a good hunt.

Day 17. You cannot change a man's behavior. Change comes from within.
Why? Do not be upset and caught up in something you cannot change. Instead, move on and smile. You deserve to be happy.

Day 18. Don't EVER make him feel he is more important than you are even if he has more education or a better job. Do not make him into a quasi-god.
Why? Never make a man a priority in your life if you are just an option in his. Always be yourself around him. If he can't accept you for your quirks, then he is not worth it.

Day 19. He is a man, nothing more, nothing less.
Why? Do not get your hopes up and do not let your guard down. Remember that if you give him a second chance, you are saying that you have forgiven his past. Do not keep holding it against him.

Day 20. Never let a man define who you are.
Why? Be amazing on your own. You might feel worthless to one person but you are priceless to another. Do not forget your value. Embrace your flaws and be true to who you really are.

Day 21. Never borrow someone else's man.
Why? Karma.

Day 22. If he cheated with you, he will cheat ON you.
Why? I will say this again. If he is willing to cheat with you, he is willing to cheat on you.

Day 23. A man will only treat you the way you ALLOW him to treat you.
Why? If he does not respect you, then you deserve better. A lady knows her limits no matter what the circumstance, stick to your guns. If you do not stand up for yourself, no one will.

Day 24. All men are NOT dogs.
Why? Do not stereotype guys; they are definitely not all the same.

Day 25. You should not be the one doing all the bending compromise is a two-way street.
Why? Remember, all limitations are self-imposed.

Day 26. **You need time to heal between relationships. There is nothing cute about baggage. Deal with your issues before pursuing a new relationship.**
Why? A man forgets but never forgives. A lady forgives but never forgets.

Day 27. **You should never look for someone to COMPLETE you. A relationship consists of two WHOLE individuals looking for someone to complement, not supplement.**
Why? Do not wait for Prince Charming to come and save you. Remember, being independent is more attractive to men. You will never find the right guy if you are looking for the wrong reasons.

Day 28. **Dating is fun even if he does not turn out to be Mr. Right.**
Why? Never lose faith in finding your perfect someone. Being single does not mean you are weak, it means you are strong enough to wait for what you really deserve. Remember just as men should not play with a woman's heart, women should not play with a man's heart either. If he does not have a chance, tell him. Do not lead him on and make him think that he has a chance when he does not.

Day 29. **Make him miss you sometimes. When a man always knows where you are and you are always readily available to him, he WILL take you for granted.**
Why? Play hard to get. Make him chase you. Be the flame, not the moth and remember the treasure does not do the hunting.

Day 30. **Do not fully commit to a man who does not give you everything that you need.**
Why? Do not fall for a guy who is not willing to catch you. Love never fails. If it fails, then it is not love.

Day 31. **Keep him in your radar but get to know others.**
Why? Flirt with him enough to show your interest, but tease him enough to make him chase you. Do not just expect to find love; wait and it will come. The moment you stop looking for something, you will find it.

50 Rules of a Sophisticated Lady

1. Be the woman a man needs, not the woman that needs a man.
2. Always accept a compliment.
3. You are beautiful and no one has the right to tell you that you're not.
4. Embrace your flaws and be true to who you really are.
5. Look like a butterfly, sting like a bee.
6. Cover up. Being a mystery is sexier than showing off every inch of your body.
7. The little black dress is a classic for a reason.
8. A real lady holds her head high but never her nose.
9. Never underestimate the power of a warm greeting.
10. For the love of decency, never chew with your mouth open.
11. True beauty comes from within.
12. Confidence is sexy.
13. Be refined, polite and well-spoken.
14. Act like a lady, think like a man.—Steve Harvey.
15. Be classy and fabulous, always.
16. Your dresses should be tight enough to show you are a woman, but loose enough to show you are a lady.
17. Arch your spine and shoulders back. This is a good posture. You are not confident until you decide to be.
18. One can never be too classy.
19. Never turn around to look back. Without doubt, he is still looking at you.
20. Beauty gets the attention but personality gets the heart.
21. You are beautiful in every single way.
22. A sincere smile is a lady's most beautiful feature.
23. It is better to be hated for who you are than be loved for someone you are not.

24. Be happy. Someone could be falling for your smile.
25. A lady should be able to make a man smile with her clothes on.
26. Talk loud enough so people can hear you but soft enough so he will have to lean in closer.
27. Being different does not mean you are uncanny. You are just a limited edition.
28. "In order to be irreplaceable, one must always be different."—Coco Chanel
29. "Always dress like you are going to see your worst enemy."—Kimora Lee Simmons
30. Leave the rumor-spreading and trash talking to Gossip Girl.
31. Always arrive at a dinner party 15 minutes late. There is nothing wrong with being fashionably late.
32. Never show you are intimidated, it shows weakness.
33. Make a man fall for your intelligence, not for your body and your double D's.
34. Always act like you are wearing an invisible crown.
35. Respect from others comes from self-respect.
36. "No one can make you feel inferior without your consent."—Eleanor Roosevelt
37. A lady should not swear. Class is defined by elegance and dignity, not by vulgar language.
38. Being intelligent is sexy; do not play stupid.
39. A lady should never throw a punch; the world is already as cruel as it is, let the universe take care of them.
40. When asked for a suggestion, do not be afraid to give your opinion. Being assertive is an attractive feature, indecisiveness is not.
41. You were born an original. Do not become a copy.
42. Laugh as much as you breathe and love as long as you live.

43. Imperfection is beauty, madness is genius. It is better to be absolutely ridiculous than absolutely boring.

44. Every day is a fashion show and the world is your runway. So always dress your best and walk with confidence.

45. Success is the best revenge.

46. Beauty is about living your life and being happy with yourself inside and out. Do not worry about what people think of you.

47. Yelling during an argument means you have already lost the fight.

48. Your smile is the sexiest curve on your entire body.

49. Be generous with expressions of gratitude such as: "Thank You" and "I appreciate that".

50. Look up the definition of sophistication. Embody it.

Money and Finance

You need to feel satisfied that your work is properly aligned with your values. This is the time to break free and redefine your path. Be careful of how you interpret your freedom and approach all decisions with caution. There will have to be serious decisions made about money, business partners, and coworkers in order to have peace in your life.

I can remember it like it was yesterday. I was the person who ridiculed everyone during Thanksgiving for going out and spending extra money because tradition says one has to have this magnificent feast or glorious spread on their dining room table in order to feel thankful. It was utterly ridiculous to me to see others run around like chickens, stripping the supermarket shelves and buying unnecessary, not to mention unhealthy food, in the spirit of Thanksgiving. I felt like a lot of people were placing unnecessary stress on themselves and people should keep it simple. Who says you need to cook all that food; I would much rather spend the extra time with family and friends.

My distaste for others actions was also a cover up for the fact that I was not a great cook. Thanksgiving always seemed like an attack on my womanhood. Even though my mother tried teaching me how to cook, I was always too busy volunteering with different organizations or participating in other various meetings, rehearsals and activities. Over the years I have learned my way around the kitchen thanks to the help of family and friends who were all older than me and felt the need to stress to me that maybe my cooking skills were the reasons why my relationships never lasted. They were definitely from the "old school" and believed that it was essential to be able to cook because supposedly the key to a man's heart was still through his stomach. The jury is still out on that theory because I know some women who can cook their butts off and their men still left or cheated on them, that is if they ever had one in the first place.

Now even though I thought they were ridiculous to still think like that in this day and time I decided that if there was any truth to what they were saying I would try to even the playing field and learn how to cook better and bake. It took some time but after days of baking dozens of cakes and pies and testing them out on friends and coworkers I even learned how to bake those pies and make homemade icing for my cakes. I was so proud; I took pictures and sent them to all of my family and friends. The subject line read, "I am woman, now hear me roar". The funny thing is I do not even like cake or pies and never ate one of them but next Thanksgiving you can bet I will be ready.

After Thanksgiving, Christmas seemed to fly by and there never seemed to be enough time to get everything done. I had managed to get my children just what they wanted and purchased small gifts for all of my friends and family. I never was used to receiving a lot for Christmas as my parents were poor growing up and everything had to be shared and divided among the five of us. Now that I am a mother, I always get some type of part time work or side job before the holidays so that I will be able to give them the gifts I never had. I went through the guilt trip of spending that money and regretting it every year until I realized that wanting to give my children nice things was not irresponsible; failing to financially prepare for those gifts was irresponsible.

All of the money I had saved up had been spent and now I was starting another year broke and financially in the red. I knew that emergencies would come up such as car problems, relatives in need, or home repairs. As a single mother, I knew I needed a savings account but it always disappeared every year because of emergencies, holidays and other unforeseen situations that arose during the year. I have heard people talking about the famous zero dollar budgeting plan which basically refers to the concept of spending every single dollar you earn in your budget spreadsheet, before the month begins. This means that every dollar in your earnings is accounted for on or before pay day. The idea is that you will assign every dollar you have to each of your expenses, even a savings account should be categorized as an expense.

I tried preparing a zero dollar budget. I planned to put aside two hundred dollars every month and then it became one hundred and soon nothing at all because of unexpected expenses that always came up and ruined my perfect spreadsheet and planning. The problem was that I was using my savings account for emergencies. Financial experts say that you should have at least three to six months of living expenses set aside in an emergency fund. I needed something practical and separate from my savings account that would fit my situation and my sometimes complicated life. I learned that I should not be using my savings account for unexpected emergencies because problems and unexpected situations will always be there and therefore I would never be able to save.

Unfortunately many people especially single mothers live paycheck to paycheck and start the beginning of the month in debt and end the month in debt trying to make sure that every day necessities like housing (rent, mortgage), transportation (car, bus, train), utilities (electric, gas, water) and food are taken care of, therefore leaving very little if any to save. I knew that I needed to start small and then grow but how would I do that not knowing how much I would be able to contribute with so many obligations and very little money.

That year I made a new year's resolution that I would set aside some money for emergency funds. I developed the C.P.R Emergency Fund especially for women and single mothers. I remember looking at my bank account and wishing for some extra zero's to magically appear on the end of my balance. That's when it hit me. I did not have a lot of money and sometimes my financial situation would change so I needed something constant, a fixed plan that I could remember and help me save as a single woman and single mother on a very small budget. I started the first month of the New Year off with the C.P.R Emergency Fund.

That year, starting with January, I added a zero so for the month of January I started my savings account with 1+0=$10. It can even be converted into a college savings plan for children. In February, representing the second month, I added another zero, 2+0=$20 and therefore adding twenty dollars to my savings account. Notice how the savings account starts growing over time in the chart. The chart was created using a simple savings calculator available on www.bankrate.com.

C.P.R Emergency Fund

Month	Amount	Balance	Widrawal Payment Plan
January	1+0=10	$10	15
February	2+0=20	$30	30
March	3+0=30	$60	45
April	4+0=40	$100	60
May	5+0=50	$150	75
June	6+0=60	$210	90
July	7+0=70	$280	105
August	8+0=80	$360	120
September	9+0=90	$450	125
October	10+0=100	$550	150
November	11+0=110	$660	165
December	12+0=120	$780	180
Happy New Year!	You did it!	$1,000 Credit Line	$1,160 Bank Loan Payoff

Simple Savings Calculator

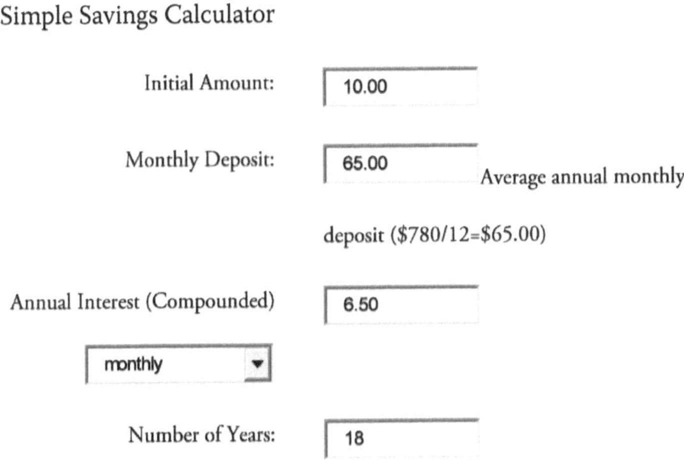

Your Results

Your average monthly deposit of $65.00 for 18 years with an average interest rate of 6.50% compounded Annually with an initial starting balance of $10.00

Year	Balance
1	$814.33
2	$1,672.53
3	$2,588.21
4	$3,565.21
5	$4,607.64
6	$5,719.88
7	$6,906.61
8	$8,172.82
9	$9,523.84
10	$10,965.33

11	$12,503.36
12	$14,144.39
13	$15,895.33
14	$17,763.53
15	$19,756.85
16	$21,883.67
17	$24,152.92
18	$26,574.15

Final Savings Balance: $26,574.15

Ninety Day Debt Repayment Plan

After you have developed a safety net through the C.P.R Emergency Fund you can now put your attention and focus toward other financial concerns like debt and unfavorable credit scores. Many of you have tons of lingering debts still haunting you and lowering your credit score and purchasing power. Merchants' use the ninety day same as cash credit plan to get your business so try using it to pay them off. Start by gathering all of the old bills you have that are less than five hundred dollars like those old cable bills before you switched to satellite or the old cell phone carrier you used to have and maybe even those pesky medical bills before you got insurance. Divide the balance by three and commit to paying them off in ninety days.

For example $500/3= $166.667. After the initial payment of $166.68 you only have two more payments to make to greater financial freedom. It is even easier if you would post date the checks or bank draft to make sure you remember your plan and obligation. You may have to do some creative budgeting like cutting back on eating out, spa days or finding ways to decrease your utility or gas expense. In the end, that is one less bill haunting you and bringing your credit score down. At the end of the year, that is a total of four bad debt bills you have eliminated from your credit report.

Name of Bill	Amount of Debt	90 day Repayment Schedule	Remaining Balance
Old Bill	$500.00	$166.68	$333.32
	$333.32	$166.66	$166.66
	$166.66	$166.66	$0

Community Calendar Plan

So what if you are fortunate to have ample financial means to support yourself or have someone support you? Then you should apply that same principle toward community involvement, charity, mentoring and volunteer hours using the Community Calendar Plan. For every numerical month, commit that amount of hours toward community involvement. For example, this year, with January representing the first month of the year, I volunteered one hour toward the charity of my choice. I started my annual community involvement, charity and volunteer hours account with one hour.

The Community Calendar Plan is an excellent plan for people or businesses that need a system in place for remembering and encouraging others to give back to the community. In February I will add two hours to my community involvement, charity, mentoring or volunteer hours. You would then continue on through the year adding an additional hour for every month of the year. Within one year, you would have contributed seventy eight hours of your time to volunteer work and helping the community. If everyone contributed at least seventy eight hours of their time every year lots of positive changes will occur everywhere in our organizations, schools, churches and other nonprofits that are all in desperate need for your help.

Community Calendar Plan

Month	Amount	Total Hours
January	1	1
February	2	3
March	3	6
April	4	10
May	5	15
June	6	21
July	7	28
August	8	36
September	9	45
October	10	55
November	11	66
December	12	78

Health: Mind, Body & Soul

Maybe some event or news turned your world upside down, making you question who you are and what you want to do with your life. Thought you had it all figured out? Maybe not and that's okay. Try to find the courage to embrace the unknown, rather than trying to mastermind and control it all. No more avoiding it: the time to deal with your baggage is NOW through deep emotional healing. I say all this with love and with the intention of pushing you into a new realm of emotional honesty. The new realm has incredible friendships, relationships, family bonds, and much more waiting for you.

Own your sneaky side that wants to get away with whatever it can. That behavior comes at a price. Your mind will fight your soul tooth and nail. Your mind will WANT to strategize, manipulate, bargain and talk your way out of this. No dice. There is only one solution and one single message: surrender. When you stop forcing and just listen, you will find yourself surrounded by divine clarity. Throughout your problem or situation you might even hear the voice of a spirit guide, guardian angel, the universe, God—whatever you want to call it. Wrap up unfinished business. FORGIVE. Stop shoving the skeletons back into the closet and invite them out for a tea party instead. They are only scary until you face them.

Ok ladies the data is in. Women everywhere, not just in the United States are not happy with their bodies. A survey of five thousand women, commissioned by REAL magazine, found that ninety one percent of women were unhappy with their bodies. In fact, a new survey has recently found that only three percent of women in the United Kingdom are totally happy with their body and seventy three percent think about their size or shape every single day. I have always been fortunate enough to have a very high metabolism, which I contribute to my ability to stay petite, so I will not pretend that I know much about weight issues and obesity struggles but I do know about the power of the mind and the need for will power.

The mind is a very powerful thing and statistics show that it takes about thirty days to make or break a habit. Even though weight was not my issue, skin problems and acne were. I believed that somehow my skin care rituals and routines must have been the reason I was experiencing such problems. No one else in my family seemed to have the skin problems except me. After trying all types of skin creams and new products I finally realized that if it was not the physical products or my personal hygiene skin care methods, then the problem must be with what I was consuming internally.

It is true that the foods we eat play a very big part on the healthiness of our bodies, the appearance of our skin, level of our confidence and therefore affecting our emotional spirit. When I became more aware of what I put into my body, I started to notice a change in the way my skin looked. The main change that I contribute to better skin was my additional water intake. I too dislike the taste of water and would prefer a Pepsi or Coke any day. It was the lack of sufficient water that was affecting the way I felt and looked both mentally and physically.

I learned how to increase my water intake slowly by using one simple method. Every time I saw or heard water

I would have to stop and drink no matter where I was or what I was doing. If I was driving in the car, I would keep a water bottle in the drink holder so if I passed by a river, lake, pool or even a sprinkler I would take a drink. If I was at home, I would keep a water bottle or glass of water in every room. If I was watching television and saw a show or commercial with water I would take a drink. If someone walked in the kitchen and turned on the faucet I would take a drink. If I was in the bathroom I would keep a bottle or glass near the sink so every time I would have to go to the bathroom to let water out, I would see that bottle or glass sitting there as I washed my hands to remind myself to put some water back in. After about thirty days I had made it a habit and I noticed the positive results in the way my body felt and looked. Now I have heard that there is research and benefits of drinking water to lose weight faster but I will not comment on that because I have no experience and I will only advise you based on what I know. My issue was skin problems but if yours is a weight problem look it up, that's what I recommend to everyone and we all know everything's on the internet.

"Like Mother, Like Daughter"

"Like mother, like daughter" is a phrase with deeper meaning than we often appreciate. For most people it means daughters resemble their mothers. Daughters will typically tend to do what their mothers did before them. There are few lifelong relationships that will ever compare to the special relationship shared between mothers and daughters. Women all over the world have a broad description of their relationship with their mothers. Some will describe their relationship as "best friends," "mortal enemies" or somewhere in between but most daughters often reach a point in their life when they realize, "I sound just like my mother."

In some respects, this is true based on the statistics below:

- If a mother smokes, her daughter is more likely to smoke.
- If a mother is unsatisfied with her body image, her daughter is more likely to be as well. In fact, mothers who diet are nearly twice as likely to have a daughter that suffers from an eating disorder.
- If a mother cohabitated, her daughter is fifty seven percent more likely to do so as well.
- If a mother is obese, her daughter is ten times more likely to be chronically overweight or obese (not due to genetics but to copying poor lifestyle choices)
- Daughters of teenage mothers are more than twice as likely to become teenage mothers themselves.

An obsession with dieting can actually cause weight gain, according to Waterhouse, a California research nutritionist. In summaries of dozens of studies and interviews, she shows how the height/weight charts have changed since the

1960s, how mothers protect their daughters from fat and thereby undernourished them and how girls, by age five, are diet-conscious. Since many women are obsessed with thinness, they diet in pursuit of their ideal body image. These women learned to diet from their mothers and will, in turn, teach their daughters by example. By age nine, 50 percent of all girls have begun restrictive diets, claims Waterhouse, author of *Outsmarting the Female Fat Cell* (1993) and *Why Women Need Chocolate* (1995).

She advocates common-sense measures such as eating a wide variety of foods in moderation, balancing food intake with exercise, and encouraging a positive body image. She offers practical suggestions for modifying eating and exercise patterns in order to achieve a healthy lifestyle. She further suggests that women are their own worst enemies. They learn their body's insecurities and disordered eating habits from their mothers and pass them on to their daughters. Women, says Waterhouse, have learned "body hatred" from a generation of moms who leaped on the Twiggy dieting bandwagon 30 years ago when self-worth was equated with weight loss.

In terms of genetics, we all know that you get half of your genes from your mom and the other half from your dad, so your mother's biology does impact your own. However, lifestyle choices, your habits, then your decisions to smoke, eat healthy, look on the sunny side of life can all influence your future as well. Similarities like those noted above are not written into your genes like your hair color or height but they are habits and tendencies that you picked up from your mom as you grow and mature.

What this means is that you may be like your mother, and if that's a positive thing in your mind then that's good. However many daughters actually fear that they will grow up to be like their mothers.

He's Your Son, NOT Your Husband

I can't tell you how many times I have heard women boasting that they do not need a man because her son was her husband. I feel so sorry for the burden these sons have to carry because of the baggage their mothers are placing on their backs. It is clear to see that these moms feel so deprived of love and attention that they turn to their sons for comfort and emotional support. These moms are either single or in a marriage that is unfulfilling or unbalanced. Unfortunately, it can lead to these boys being incapable of having mature, loving and healthy balanced adult relationships because they will constantly have to support and comfort their mothers.

So how can a son divorce his mother without the guilt trip? In the beginning, there must be boundaries. Sons' should have boundaries in their relationship with their mothers and mothers should have boundaries in their relationship with their sons. You are the adult, so be consistent with being the adult. Once you involve your son in personal matters or leave him to make adult decisions, you have placed him in the position of authority. If you tell him, he is the man of house, he will take it literally. Understand your son is not your equal. He's not your support system; you are supposed to be his support. Conflict will eventually arise later if you bring in a boyfriend.

Get a life of your own. If your marriage is unfulfilling, do something about it. You should be able to talk and share with your spouse, not your son. If you decide to make him your marriage counselor, do not be surprised if he starts to resent his father. If you are single, rely on your friends and family for emotional support or get counseling if you need it.

Bottom line let your son live his life.

(C.P.R) Learn How to Choose, Prepare, and React

My purpose is to resuscitate and breathe life into that exceptional woman you know personally that has recently gone through an exceptional difficult situation in their life. They need to know that there is still hope for joy and that life has allowed this exceptional situation to happen to them. They may truly be an exceptional person and exceptional people are always exceptional in everything they do. When they do anything good they are exceptionally well at it. When they do wrong things, they do them exceptionally bad. When they are feeling good, they get exceptionally happy and when they get upset they get exceptionally angry. They have no middle ground or balance because things in their life are usually going exceptionally good or exceptionally bad.

Unfortunately we all seem to have to walk through the ring of fire in times of trouble and hardship, falling deeply into what seems to be an eternal pit of despair. Learn how to apply C.P.R to all of life's daily challenges by choosing your battles wisely, preparing your mind for the test of life and reacting only after evaluating every thought, action and consequence. Through C.P.R you will be able to revive your mind, body, soul and spirit and pursue life with joy and happiness.

Learn how to find balance because exceptional people do exist in this world and they have to learn a complicated technique called, "Mind over Matter". It is about learning how to train your mind to consider what really matters to you. You must highlight the importance of living and learning through assessing the problems you will go through in life and growing mentally as a result of your life challenges. Believe it or not this starts with birth. Your birth may not be when you were physically born in the world but when you first were able to open your eyes and see life through a set of brand new eyes or lenses as you have never been able to see things before.

The period before your new birth is the gestation phase. Gestation is the period between when a seed has been planted, beginning with fertilization and ending in your new birth. During life's gestation phase your problems will feed you, helping you to grow and then you will eventually, inevitably, develop insight and knowledge through experience which nurtures your mind, body and spirit. By practicing (C.P.R); Choosing wisely, Preparing your mind and Reacting positively to life's challenges you will be well equipped to navigate the road of life and become resistant to its many challenges and detours.

(C) Choose

Every person creates his life through life choices. One of the wonderful gifts that the Lord gave the human race is "Free Moral Will", or in other words the right to make your own *choices* or decisions. Our *choices* affect our mood and the way we feel about ourselves and this is the law of cause and effect. No action goes unnoticed. Every aspect of your life comes under two categories: things that you are at cause over and things that are the effect of your decision. You can be at cause over your job, family or relationships.

After you have chosen your path and experienced a few detours in life you have now become accustomed to stopping to smell the flowers along the way. There is nothing wrong with stopping to enjoy some of life's luxuries but it can become very tempting to pick them up and bring them along with you through life's journey. If you continue to do this in life, your journey will be very long and may seem heavier along the way. Sometimes in life there will be things, people and situations that you will have to adopt a "look but do not touch" mentality. Learn how to admire but leave them right where they are as you continue on your journey.

"To everything there is a season and a time to every purpose under the heavens." Ecclesiastes 3:1. God has timing by which He flows. What is He calling you to do? Are you confused? If so, not to worry for it is just a season. There may be a problem with agitation, confrontation and battle. "He has made everything beautiful in His time." Ecclesiastes 3:11. God created everything with a purpose. It takes time to establish a proven record of integrity which God possesses. It will take time to extract information or lessons from a crisis. It takes time to be restored when you have made a major mistake. If you tried to bring forth fruit out of season, all it will bring is death and destruction.

Learn to see and step out of the box. Jesus could not do many miracles in his own town because people only knew him as Mary's son. He knew he had to leave home in order to be heard and seen as he preached God's word. They had put him into a box and when people put you into a box their visions, thoughts and reasoning are affected.

"The steps of a good man are ordered by the Lord and He is delighted in His way." Psalm 37:23. If you find that people have placed you in a box and feel that you are caught in a current just go with the current and do not fight it. Blessed is the man that walketh not in the counsel of the ungodly, nor standeth in the way of sinners nor sitteth in the seat of the scornful. You have to listen, learn patience and learn how to recognize your season. Your situation may not look good at the moment but there still can be peace. If you want your prayers answered just pray the word and God will always give you a way out or a way to escape. When you are blinded by a problem, sometimes you cannot see the escape given to you by God.

Peaceful Sleep

"For as a man thinketh, so is his heart and so is he." Proverbs 23:7. A negative mind will equal a negative life. You must renew your mind daily. There are two parts of the mind; the conscious mind and the subconscious mind. The conscious mind is the part that controls your thinking and reasoning. The subconscious mind controls our beliefs, attitudes, emotions and memory. Your thoughts control your mind and your mind controls your actions. Learn to control your thoughts and bring every thought into captivity.

A double minded man is back and forth on opinions and decisions. He is unstable in all His ways and cannot receive anything from the Lord. God says His word will never return to Him void, and it will do exactly what it says it will do. You must not allow yourself to become a slave to bitterness. Bitterness will enslave you, wipe the smile off of your face and drain your soul and spirit. Regardless of what made you bitter you need to overcome it because bitterness will rob you of success and joy.

Ten Steps to Overcome Bitterness

1. Admit that you are living with bitterness.
2. Admit that it is wrong and damaging.
3. Stay in harmony with Godly friends.
4. Look for the lesson the Holy Spirit wants to teach.
5. Do not speak your bitterness to others. The Bible says "put off the former conversation." Ephesians 4:29. Let not corrupt conversation proceed out of your mouth but that which is good for edifying the person. If you are going to think on anything, think on good things. Administer grace not damnation to others. Pharaoh cursed Moses and it returned to him. Watch what you say and do because it can return unto you.
6. Soak your soul, passions, will and memories in the scripture. Visit the Psalms of David who learned how to cry to the Lord.
7. Plan new projects in your future; do something new.
8. Think ahead not backwards. Stop living in the past. Your past is ruining the future because you cannot move beyond it. Do not get caught up on the memories of the past by holding on to them and delaying the blessings of the future. Many have said they wanted to move beyond where they are but their mind stays stuck in the past.
9. Study winners in the Bible. Joseph's brothers did him wrong by selling him so that he would miss his blessing. Joseph did not seek revenge or bring down the hammer on them. He came out the real winner overall.
10. Discuss with the Holy Spirit. He will choke out those thoughts.

Remember your mouth tells your mind what to do. Pray out loud. Faith comes by hearing. Your mouth speaks your future. God said, "This day I call heaven and earth, life and death, blessings and curses." Deuteronomy 30:19. "Now you choose which one you want to follow. Whatever you learn, seen, heard from me put into practice and peace shall follow." Philippians 4:9.

Wondering why you are struggling. Quit robbing God and trying to be blessed because if you sow, you shall weep. Do not allow people around you who are failing in the area that you are looking for counseling. When you seek counsel with these people most of the time you will get cosigners to your wrong doings. Follow someone who has some truth and knowledge both spiritually and financially. Give these people double honor who preach doctrine, wisdom, scripture and the word of God. You must have an example you can see.

Struggle of the Flesh

Sometimes after bad relationships we are feeling arrogant, hurt and even vengeful. Loneliness may set in and there are hot passions in us that we may find ourselves unwilling and unable to control. This is when we must muster up strength and learn to tame the lion or beast within like Daniel in the lion's den. It is wild and fierce but this passion can be banked, like a fire in a hearth. Let them run wild and they will do damage. You need to develop true strength. To do that, you need to learn to balance everything in you that is human, animal and divine. It may seem impossible but love, kindness and the word of God can bring those passions into balance. Your higher nature can triumph over material, emotional and physical desire.

In John 4:4 remember the woman at the well, there was a Samaritan woman whose issues were deeper than her immorality, failed marriages and promiscuity. The woman went to the well in the sixth hour of the evening when she knew no one would be there because normally people would fetch water in the early morning. We may conclude that she was trying to avoid men. We can get away from the issue but we can't get away from the frustration. Until you get that issue or that inner craving under control you will never be satisfied and always thirsty. Jesus told the woman at the well that anyone that drinks of the water that Jesus gives him will never be thirsty again and will become in him a spring of water welling up to eternal life.

"We know that the law is spiritual; but I am unspiritual sold as a slave to sin." Romans 7:14-25. If you want the blessing you got to have the struggle. You must struggle to do right in the midst of evil. The struggle is in the flesh. God said that out of your struggle He will raise you up and bless your life so before you can be delivered you have to deal with yourself.

It may be that you are not bearing your cross and you are not ready for your blessing. For when you are ready, your blessings will flow. Confess and clean up your mess. Ezekiel 14:14. Wonder how people's secrets always manage to come out. Somehow, someway they are exposed by some minor detail they forgot to omit, overlook or cover up. No matter the secret, from embezzlement, crimes, love affairs or the discovery of a secret love child, it will always come out. Call on God and confess while He may be found or reconcile with that someone special before you are exposed. Remember everything done in the dark always comes to the light and God's word will never return void so get it right today.

Spirit of Discontentment

Some people have a spirit of discontentment and are never satisfied. Are people just worshipping the package and really not loving you. If you receive this truth, it will set you free. So you are unhappy with what you have or who you are with. You get another or something new and see how long it takes before you get tired of it because you are always changing. The problem is not them, it is you. You keep changing, flipping and flopping trying to find satisfaction.

When you are never satisfied you will wreck every relationship or everything you come into contact with but when you get a relationship with God, He will make you feel that the one you are with or the thing you have is everything. A spirit of discontentment has nothing to do with the people it comes from your heart and your spirit. Often we are begging and looking for validation, and acknowledgements. That is how the enemy can seduce you with what you did not get or believe you do not have. He will seduce you with what you complain about the most. Remember you cannot seduce a full man when he is not hungry and temptation is born out of hunger and thirst.

Gain is defined as what you have left over. You get out of life what you put in it so invest and put stock into your relationships. It is easy for people to have ten years of work and profit under their belt but be emotionally empty. Therefore after all that hard work you have gained nothing. In the Bible Paul said, "I have had experiences enough in life and I have learned that whatever state I am in I will be content." Your condition is not the end of the story so just learn to be content in the present state you are in for the bible says "this too shall pass." This situation is not how your story will end and it is only a temporary situation.

Spirit of Infirmity

Try your best to live clean and holy. When you are so anointed by the spirit of the living God everyone and everything around you will come into order. Form a contract with God and say, "Here is my exchange Lord, let me give you what you need." Often times when a string of bad things start happening in your life there is a place or a point you can trace back where everything went wrong. You must learn to understand and break the cycle of infirmity in your life. You should be comforted in knowing that the spirit of God is transferable.

Greater is God that is in me than he that is in the world. Jesus did not leave you money in the bank He left you His spirit. God will show up in the spirit of what you need. If you are lonely He shows up in the spirit of company. If you are confused He will come in the spirit of peace. If I need anything I must believe God will give it to me. If He does not give it to me, then it must not be good for me. God knows if that thing is good for you. God says that He will not withhold anything good from you and you must continue to walk upright. The problem is most of us can't live or walk upright long enough to get the good thing God has for us. Do not try to live ten different lives and call on the Lord. He is not your butler where you can call Him when you want and dismiss Him when you are finished with Him.

(P) Prepare

Are you ready to quit that bad habit and get rid of that addiction? It does not matter if it is an emotional or physical dependency you are trying to let go of because they both will require lots of determination, strength and effort. You have to be *prepared* to do what it takes to succeed. *Prepare* your mind for action, be self-controlled and keep sober in spirit. Fix your hope completely on the grace and answer that will be revealed to you. (1 Peter 1:13). Call it what you will. Prayer, meditation, centering down, moment of silence, whatever, just consider it done.

Get your mind into position. When God breaks a yoke in your life He will not withhold anything good from you. Get your life right then you will know that your lifestyle is not the reason why He is withholding that thing from you and if He still withholds that thing from you, Gods knows that it must not be good for you. Every good gift and every perfect gift is from above and cometh down from the father. James 1:17.

Stop trying to force things like relationships especially when you know it is not working. It is like that sesame street song, "one of things is not like the other and one of things does not belong here." Let it go and if it comes back it will mean so much more. Ephesians 1:5-6 mentions that God makes provisions through a problem. What may look like a mess is really a blessing. What you thought was a curse may turn out to be a blessing. When God begins to move in your life, you have to have a level of discern that He is doing something powerful in your life. Remember the story of Elijah; when God got ready to bless him with food He sent a nasty raven with bread in his mouth. Do not miss your blessing because you are more concerned with the vessel and what you want it to look like instead of a mighty gift from God. As for me and my house I say "Anyway you want to bless me Lord, bless me and I will be satisfied."

Some people continue to stay in out dated, unhealthy situations because it is familiar and feels safe. You must allow yourself to be led out blind and stop determining when and where you are going to use faith. Never make a permanent decision based on a temporary situation. Ask yourself, "Why am I making this decision on unclear information?" Surround yourself with people that can see clearly and can help you see clearly.

In order to see clearly where you want to be and where you want to go you must have a vision. There is power in vision because anything that affects your vision affects your mobility. God told Moses to tell Pharaoh, "Let my people go." Moses spoke about his limitations which was his stuttering problem. God's vision is always bigger than what you think you can do or handle. As your perception clears your dependency and stock you put into other people will diminish. Speak to your situation and get out of your limitations. Moses had to learn to keep it together, keep the faith and wait for his appointed time.

You are responsible for guarding your mind. Behind everything you do there is a thought behind it first. If you are serious about changing your life then change how you think. We have a tendency to blame everybody else about our situation. Changing is a process and you must renew your mind daily with the word of God so combat the enemy by speaking the word.

Change always begins in your mind. You cannot think on negative things and receive good things in return. Good thoughts bring good things and bad thoughts bring bad things. Your mind will lead you to negative thinking and eventually your body will follow. Thoughts will eventually become action so align your mind like you align your car or it will start driving rough and veering off to the side of the road. Change your thoughts now before you find yourself and life off course, heading towards things you did not intend to get into or places you did not intend to go.

When we go through circumstances we will have to remind ourselves and train our thoughts to believe that we already have the victory. We are flesh on the outside but we have the spirit of God on the inside. Sometimes you have to remember that you are going through not just for you but maybe for someone else down the road that may also be going through the same thing and needs to hear your testimony. Learn to trust in God and in due season, God will bring you out. Recognize that we are in a spiritual warfare and the battlefield is in our minds. If Satan can put thoughts into our mind, then he can control our actions. Take up your armor which is the word of God and practice fasting. Every thought you entertain either has a life or death sentence attached to it because if acted upon it may bring forth a life or death result to the situation.

Sometimes God is arranging some things for you and you must go through some things in order for God to use you. You have to be balanced in life. No matter your age you will go through struggles and betrayals. Even Jesus suffered from struggles and betrayal with his disciples. God will shield you and keep you hidden where he wants you until he is ready to release you. Remember the story of Moses who he kept hidden and safe until he was ready to use him to lead the people. When you are ready and anointed it does not have to be announced. The anointed will show because you will be blessed and highly favored.

Suffering can be a result of the loss or lack of ministry and we must be taught to withstand suffering. After you have suffered for a while God will bring you forth like pure gold. Stop complaining under your suffering. In your families establish and follow order. Remember God speaks to the man and women should study to keep their mouth closed. Teach your children how to wait and how to suffer. Sometimes people can develop mental, physical and emotional illnesses because they have never been taught the concept of suffering.

Rejoice through your suffering. Until you are rejected you will not be delivered. Be happy and shout hallelujah anyhow. Satan is smart and he will use people you love instead of your enemies to get you out of God's will. The devil knows you are too wise to listen or follow an enemy so he uses people that are close to you like friends and family members to get you to participate in wrong doing.

Keeping the Faith

I heard a very spiritual apostle once say that faith is the most potent force in the universe because it confers divinity upon humanity. It took some meditation but now I know that faith draws on the power of God. Your wailing and crying does not invoke the power of God. God does not honor you. He honors His word and His word is above His name. Your faith is the spiritual platform for the power of God. What have you done this week by faith? Where are your bruises? Get in the word and find a scripture for your dilemma. Stop crying about your troubles.

Remember the story of Jesus on the boat in the storm. It was no normal storm because this storm came out of nowhere. Jesus rose up and said "Peace be still." This is God using Jesus to assert His power of Lord over nature. We have all witnessed this power throughout the world by unexplained events like miraculous healings and stories of survival. How tornadoes and hurricanes can whip through entire villages leaving a single home untouched. Or when God's people were hungry and Jesus asked a little boy for his meal. Jesus blessed the meal and fed over five thousand people. He is a God of resources, so if you give it to him he will bless and multiply it. God is the ruler of all things and when you move closer to God he begins to bless you.

When you move away from God's presence you begin to do what is right in your own eyes. You cannot walk close to God and do what you want at the same time. You must have accountability and conviction in your life through realization of what you have done. Remember when you belong to God, He will always give you a way of escape. This is His way of calling you out of your hoggish lifestyle according to His own time and itinerary.

Unfortunately, there are hoggish lifestyles all around us. There are the downright low down hoggish lifestyles of those that have very messy lives. They do not want to do any better and are living hand to mouth every day. Next are our everyday hoggish people who are lying, fornicating, cheating and committing adultery by lying up all day having sex with whomever and whenever they want. The hog always has others out there and you are just one of many. Then you have your church folk who also have hoggish lifestyles but they are just a little more dignified with theirs. They too are messy, selfish, have bad credit, do not pay their bills on time, trying to keep up with the Jones's, married but still messy. Stop living among hoggish, messy, and dead people in your community.

Some people feel that it is the hoggish church folk that keep them away from the church. Do away with people of the world and their traditions. Your traditions make God's word of no effect and make it so hard for God's people to come to him and hear his word. They have rules about proper dress, whether or not we should have drums, recognizing elders, ministers, deacons, bishops and what pew or side of the church belongs to whom. We want titles on our names in order to do something. You can have a title and still live an unholy hoggish life. Any role that is not universal is not God because when God gives truth he gives it to all men. Stop trying to make a doctrine out of something you do not even do.

If any man be in Christ Jesus all things are passed. Jesus did not need attention. His miracles spoke for him. Remember he fed thousands with two fish and five loaves of bread, turned water into wine, and performed resurrections. Mary, Martha and Lazarus were friends of Jesus and they had a special relationship with him. They felt that if Jesus would have been there then their brother would not have died. In Jesus tradition three days had passed and the power or hope to resurrect the dead was lost on the fourth day. Jesus showed up on the fourth day after Lazarus body had begun to decay. Many said that it was too late but Jesus simply said, "Show me where he lay." There is nothing impossible for God! Lazarus was walking around as a living, breathing testimony of God's power.

You can be doing everything just right and something will come up and attack your purpose. You must tell yourself that the situation will be alright because though the answer may tarry, you must wait on the Lord. Have faith that He will see you through your situation. Faith comes by hearing the word of God. Faith is the substance of things hoped for and the evidence of things not seen. There must be something you want or are after in order for money to be needed otherwise what good is it unless you can spend it. Faith works the same way. It has to get down inside your heart and in your spirit where you believe God will fix it for you. Though the vision tarries, wait for it shall speak in the end and it will not lie.

Values for Godly Women

Faith

The first value is faith. Then Jesus answered, "Woman, you have great faith! Your request is granted." And her daughter was healed from that very hour. (Matthew 15:28)

Now faith is the substance of things hoped for, the evidence of things not seen. (Hebrews 11:1 KJV)

For we walk by faith, not by sight. (2 Corinthians 5:7 KJV)

But without faith it is impossible to please him: for he that cometh to God must believe that he is, and that he is a rewarder of them that diligently seek him. (Hebrews 11:6 KJV)

Divine Nature

The next value to discuss is Divine Nature. The scripture is 2 Peter 1:4-7. The motto for this value is "I have inherited divine qualities, which I will strive to develop." This is a wonderful value for women to learn about and focus on.

Knowledge

For God giveth to a man that is good in his sight wisdom, and knowledge, and joy: but to the sinner he giveth travail, to gather and to heap up, that he may give to him that is good before God. This also is vanity and vexation of spirit. (Ecclesiastes 2:26 KJV)

For the LORD giveth wisdom: out of his mouth cometh knowledge and understanding. He layeth up sound wisdom for the righteous: he is a buckler to them that walk uprightly.

He keepeth the paths of judgment, and preserveth the way of his saints. (Proverbs 2:6-8 KJV)

Good Works

Let your light so shine before men, that they may see your good works, and glorify your Father which is in heaven. (Matthew 5:16)

Integrity

Then his wife said to him, "Do you still hold fast your integrity? Curse God and die." Job 2:9.

Far be it from me That I should say you are right; Till I die I will not put away my integrity from me. I hold fast my righteousness and will not let it go; my heart does not reproach me for any of my days. (Job 27:5-6)

I think that Job truly did trust in God. He knew serving God was right. He had fear and love for God, so even throughout all he went through; he was able to remain faithful to god through it all. He serves as a great example as to how we should each live.

Individual Worth

The next value is Individual Worth. The scripture is "Remember the worth of souls is great in the sight of God" (Doctrine and Covenants 18:10). This theme focuses on self-esteem. Women should know that the Heavenly Father loves each of us and that He is aware of us and our needs. Set your sights on the heavens and fly like an eagle. Eagles do not socialize with buzzards.

Choice and Accountability

And if it seems evil unto you to serve the LORD, choose you this day whom ye will serve; whether the gods which your fathers served that were on the other side of the flood, or the gods of the Amorites, in whose land ye dwell: but as for me and my house, we will serve the LORD. (Joshua 24:15)

Virtue

Who can find a virtuous woman? For her price is far above rubies. (Proverbs 31:10)

God's Word Sets the Standard for Morality. Virtue is moral excellence. God is absolute virtue (excellence, 2 Pet. 1:3). Therefore, God sets the standard for virtue. Since God has given us all things that pertain to life and godliness (2 Pet. 1:3), He has given us the standard for moral excellence in His word (2 Tim. 3:16-17).

Society dictates neither morality nor virtue. We cannot live by the world's standard of morality and expect to go to heaven (Is. 55:8-9; 1 Cor. 1:18f). A virtuous life is the result of hearing God's word, believing God's word, and obeying God's word (Rom. 10:17; Heb. 5:9). When we live according to the law and doctrine of Christ, we are virtuous (Gal. 6:2; Col. 3:17; 2 Jn. 1:9).

Pressing Your Way Through

God is the ruler of all things. When you move away from God, demonic people start to feel comfortable around you. They invite you in, accepting you because they feel you are one of them now. Remember the story of the man who lived outside of town and was afflicted and tormented with demons, when he heard of Jesus arrival he pressed his way to Jesus and fell to his knees. He commanded the demons name and the demon answered, "I am Legion." The demons recognized a higher power and authority and even they had to come into order. Jesus commanded the demons out of the man and they ran into the swine. It does not matter what the demon in your life is, when Jesus comes onto the scene even your demons will come into order and get in line.

It is in you to be blessed. Ephesians 1:3-9. Pray for your daily bread and do not worry about worries and concerns of tomorrow and next month. Seek him why he may be found and while he is near. I do not want to miss today looking for tomorrow. We have the word everywhere today but is the word in us? Do you have an appetite for God or for the world? He will not force feed you but He will go to and fro throughout the earth looking for someone to bless. God is looking for people that are hungry. It is the vanity of riches why people forfeit happiness for something they think they want only to find out it is not what they really wanted after all. You must have an appetite for God because he does not feed people who are not hungry.

Learn how to enjoy God's purpose for your life. You have to also develop an appetite for God's purpose. Learn how to give God the glory even in your struggle. Stop holding back from God and surrender it all by denying yourself. Do not seek your own happiness first, seek God and He will give you everything else you are working so hard to get. Seek first the kingdom of God and all good things will be added unto you.

You must confess that you are hungry for God in your life. People are turning their heads away from the powerful move of God. God wants to see some pressing through your hardships. Through the pressing He will strengthen you. Learn to press your way through your problems in life.

(R) React

Have you ever gone about your day feeling happy and carefree, when all of sudden something sneaks up on you—a trigger—that stirs you up and throws you for a loop? Change your *Reaction*, change your life. What you can change is your *reaction* to what you encounter, and then your life will begin to change. Most people spend their lives in a negative *reaction*. How can you get rid of the negative *reactions* and emotional drama in your life? Stop emotional *reactions* and change your core beliefs.

You can have happiness through self-awareness. What are your emotional triggers? Discovering your emotional triggers provide opportunities for self discovery and will allow you to decide how you want to show up to the world. The strengths that have helped you to succeed are also your greatest emotional triggers when you feel someone is not honoring what makes you happy. Transitions in life may not always feel like a good thing, but you can make it through change with grace instead of grief.

When we have a dream, goal, idea, hope, wish or desire, we have to be more like farmers. We need to take our precious seed or desire and plant it in prepared, healthy soil. Your healthy soil is a balanced life that is full of faith, love and lots of nurturing. Nurture your life with positive things that give you joy and happiness. Positive things in your life will always bestow blessings unto you like a never ending, magical spring of water. Seek out those people or things that can water you, or nurture you for it will be those people or things that will make the greatest impact on your life.

Even though we all need to be nurtured, and loved sometimes the one thing we need most is to be left alone for the magic of gestation to take place. Once we plant our seed, we have to resist the urge to micromanage it. How well do you think a sunflower would do if we dug up the seed everyday and asked it, "Have you grown yet?" The next time you find yourself frustrated because your desire has not manifested, remind yourself that it has not manifested YET and a solution it is on it way. Your unresolved problem is in its gestation phase and an answer will arrive when it and you are ready. Trust the process.

Remember Dorothy from the 1939 movie The Wizard of Oz, she too was on a spiritual journey. She grew up an orphan and was always searching for her true home. It was only through a major crisis or when someone threatened to take her precious and closest companion away did she embark on her journey. She then got caught up in a tornado, a whirlwind of different people and situations that came into her life to symbolize how she must figure out what mattered to her. What were her true feelings and inspiration in life? She meets up with a wise woman who gives her direction and tells her to "follow the yellow brick road."

The yellow brick road served as Dorothy's mantra on her journey and she should never let go of her ruby slippers which represents her inner spirit, that inner self, spark and true you. Along her journey she meets up with a scarecrow that has a head but no brain, the tin man who has a chest but no heart, and the cowardly lion who represents power but no courage. All of these characters represent a part of her soul, thoughts, feelings and free will. Dorothy had to learn to live and operate through life. All of us have a little Dorothy in us and we have to learn to overcome life challenges to achieve self realization. The Bible will serve as your mantra or guide through your journey.

Gerald's Journey

Gerald lived in a little a small, rural, southern town in Conboard, South Carolina. Even though it was a very small town with only one caution light it was very busy because it also happened to be the county seat. Conboard was home to the courthouse, post office, town hall, library, bank and other small offices which are all located on the same street.

Nothing really went on in these buildings but the day to day talk, taxes and gossip. Every day you would see the locals sitting, chatting away on the courthouse steps and occasionally rising to greet the county judge, major, police officers and other officials that walked by. Nothing ever seemed to change in Conboard. It did not matter if you were gone two years or twenty years, every building, tree and sign remained exactly where it had always been before. You could return on any given day and still find the locals sitting on the courthouse step, speaking and greeting every passerby with kindness and warmth.

Gerald's mother was a beautiful woman with long black hair. She was also from Conboard but he lived on the outskirts of town in a little community called Bottleneck. Bottleneck was not connected to the main road at that time and it was an hour ride by horse to Conboard back then.

Gerald was the youngest of six children born to his parents and they had a very hard life, as did everyone in those times. Gerald was grown now but his earliest memories of his father would be of him sweeping the sidewalk every Sunday afternoon after church. He was a very clean man and each day he would have on a crisp, clean white shirt which baffled Gerald because he never understood why his father would wear a white shirt if his daily task involved working with his hands, sweeping, working in the garden or on his farm.

When family would come over to visit, his father would ask his mother to fix something for the guest to eat. She would gripe and complain but do it anyway. The main course was always homemade bread or biscuits which she served with jelly, honey, molasses, cheese, or whatever they had in the pantry at that time. It was always good, tasty, sweet and always seemed to be enough to put a smile on everyone's face. Gerald remembered how his mother was always moving around never sitting still and always busy doing something around the house like a robot because she felt it was expected of her as a wife and mother. As she worked in the house she would be yelling and giving orders all at the same time while still moving about cleaning, folding and cooking. She was very happy when Gerald grew up and came home to visit. He would just sit and talk with her for hours.

After Gerald's father died she slowed down and did not much moving around anymore. When he passed away she spent the rest of her days sitting on the porch watching traffic go by and swatting the bugs away. She always wore a skirt or dresses her entire life because women of her time never wore pants. She could always be found sitting on her porch and had a towel in her lap which covered up her legs. It was not until she died of a blood disorder did Gerald realize that she had been suffering from an infection that turned into gangrene in her legs. He was very sad and felt guilty because he had never bothered to ask why she kept her legs covered all the time.

After both of his parents died Gerald never cried or appeared sad. It was odd that he seemed to be the most mature, yet he was the youngest of all of his brothers and sisters. Even though Gerald had five other siblings, he was the only one close to his parents. Gerald was born with a learning disability and as a result he developed a speech problem. One of his brothers died when he was young, his sister ran away when she was thirteen and no one has heard from her since.

His brother William, however, was the poster child for popularity and entertainment. He loved performing for people and they considered him to a wonderful guitarist and musician. His brother Larry was the middle brother and considered the comedian of the bunch. He was a carefree, no worry guy that like having a good time and wanted everyone around him to have a good time too. Larry did not have to speak; he had a way of just looking at you and could brighten up your day.

Then there was his sister Beverly, always fashionably dressed in red because she loved attention. They called her "sister" and she was slick in the mouth, always on the move and fast-footed. Gerald loved when she came to visit. She seemed to know how to do everything and it appeared like she lived out of her suitcase because she was always on the go. She would come home to visit and be able to clean Gerald's entire house from top to bottom and cook and still find time to meet and greet with old friends and neighbors. Gerald would go hunting and Beverly would find time to cook the best deer stew known to man. She would get everybody all riled up and excited but then be off again leaving a wake in her absence and a trail of sad puppy dogs behind her.

Gerald had such good times when William or Beverly came to visit. They had a flare for fun and entertainment, but music was there passion. After a big brawl or uproar about nothing they would all be caught laughing again and having a great time. All of them were musically talented whether it was on the harmonica, guitar or singing. When they came home, a party was sure to follow.

William was Gerald's favorite brother and he would light up when he would come home to visit. Gerald was never much of a talker but when his brother William came to visit it seemed like he would awaken out of a deep sleep. He did not come home to visit often maybe about every three or four years but he made up for every moment that he was gone. It was only when William visited that Gerald would play the guitar. He would laugh and make up songs encouraging everyone to join in and perform with them. Gerald and William were about ten years apart in age and William would stand tall over Gerald like a puppet master. Gerald would willingly move along and do whatever William wanted him to do. When William would leave Gerald used to sit quiet, alone, and sad until his brother returned home again.

Leila's Journey

Leila was one out of nine children born in 1952 to Carter and Beulah who were a wealthy couple that owned and farmed their own land. Carter and Beulah owned several acres of land on the outskirts of Conboard and it was called the Dowls Plantation. It is still called the "Dowls Plantation" today and it is still where a lot of the family members reside. It was a happy place until the winter of 1958 when Beulah died giving birth to a baby boy.

Out of the nine children, two of the older children Bethany who was age nineteen and John who was age seventeen left home. They moved out of town and set out on their own. The oldest daughter Dorothy got married and moved to New York City. Her new husband did not treat her well but for her he was a way out and an escape from the sadness at home. She was no stranger to hard work because she had constantly been a helper to her mom through the years in the house as well as on the farm. She quickly found a job at the post office and began to provide for herself. Later she left her abusive husband and maintains her independence.

John the oldest son got a job as an electrician apprentice for the state utility company. It was he who was able to help get my mom an administrative job at the utility company later on after she graduated from college. He also quickly married and started a family with a local hair dresser named Samantha. He was considered a catch by the ladies at that time and his wife considered herself lucky to have found such an eligible hard working man during those times. Ten years and three kids later Samantha decided to call it quits on John and left him. I guess that did not bother him because he soon found another wife. Men then were no different from several of the men today because he found a new wife was more beautiful and much younger, sixteen years old to be exact. Her name was Stacy and she was well liked because she sparkled and shined wherever she went, lighting up the room and the atmosphere. They married quickly after Johns' divorce from Samantha but their marriage also ended ten years and four kids later.

After Bethany and John moved away, seven children were left on the farm. Their father Carter was a traditional man and he had no clue about how to raise or take care of children. Carter split up the children and they were all sent to different aunts and uncles that had the heart to take some of the siblings into their homes and raise them. He was very sad about having to send the children away to relatives and split them up but he knew that he would have to, in order to be able to keep and work his farm. So he sent four of them—Daisy age fifteen, Elroy age thirteen, Paul age eleven, and Faye age nine to live with his late wife's sister who also lived in Bottleneck.

Leila at age six was sent to live with her Aunt Bee in the city of Conboard. Carly, the youngest daughter was three years old and Tom the baby boy whose childbirth resulted in the death of their mother were sent to live with their grandmother who was very sad at the death of her daughter Beulah. She had spoken to her son-in-law Carter and told him that she would keep the youngest two who she considered still babies and did not trust anyone else to look after. Their grandmother Mary had eighteen children of her own and twelve of them still lived at home but kept her word and took in the smallest two who were just babies at the time of her daughters' death. Word had spread around the community about her hardship and perseverance with all fourteen children. Everyone would comment throughout the community about the neatness and smartness of the children. She was often praised for her love, compassion and care of the children.

Leilas' caregiver, Aunt Bee was considered to be very well off for she was an educator in the school system and owned her own house. She wore the finest clothes and ate on the finest china. Something most people, especially single women were not able to do at that time. She resided in a colonial home located behind the courthouse that she was purchasing from one of the officials who hired her to teach. She worked so hard in life and never found the opportunity to marry or have children. So when the opportunity to raise Leila came along, she was excited and joyous that she now had the opportunity to raise a child. When Leila was brought to her aunts' house to stay by her father she was very sad so he promised to visit her often as well as make sure she got a chance to play with her brothers and sisters. Leila only got that chance to play with them on every first and third Sunday after church as they all attended the same family church on the outskirts of town between Conboard and Bottleneck. Through the years the play dates together dwindled as sometimes one or more of the children would miss church and they never seemed to be able to get together all at once except for holidays.

Aunt Bee spent her entire life making sure she was as close to perfection as she could be. She raised Leila very well and made sure she had the best opportunities and exposure available to little girls at that time. She taught Leila what she deemed to be the important things in life. She taught her the crafts of cooking, sewing, and knowledge about fine draperies, china and etiquette. Leila wore the best dresses, shoes and was taught everything about how to live, eat, walk and talk in proper society.

People would always say that Leila was someone special and represented young women very well during her early adult years. She was considered a very independent, beautiful woman and owned her own house and her own car. Leila had a college degree in office administration and was able to work as an administrative secretary for the utility company at that time thanks to the help of her brother John.

Leila was doing very well for herself in the eyes of all that observed her. She could easily be spotted riding through town in her brand new car. She was well liked by others and was well respected in the community by neighbors, friends and had plenty of potential suitors. There were several young men in the community that believed that Leila was the cream of the crop when it came to looking for a wife. Leila was not interested in the role of wife and mother as she had been taught the value of independence and how to take care of herself. She continued to serve in the community, church and work while still caring for Aunt Bee who was now in old age.

Leila seemed to have everything in life but was not happy because all of the friends that she grew up with were off getting married and having children. Soon all of the potential suitors who were interested in Leila had moved on and selected other women who seemed more interested in the role of wife and mother. Most women then were stay at home moms and Leila found herself having less in common and nothing to talk about with her friends that she seemed so close to.

Leila missed the days when she and her friends could go to church together, dinner and out to the movies especially with her friends Cheryl and Maxine who were twin sisters. The three of them had been connected at the hip since they were little girls. Cheryl and Maxine were not as financially well off and did not have a wealthy aunt like Leila. That never mattered to Leila who never seemed to care when she used to visit and play with the twins in their small four room house with an outhouse out back. Cheryl was quiet and reserved while Maxine was full of cheer and the daredevil of the two. Maxine was constantly up to something and could always be counted on for a laugh.

Cheryl and Maxine's mother may have been poor but she made sure her girls were neat and clean. She loved to sew and would make them the cutest dresses to wear. When they were little girls people thought they were triplets skipping through town because Leilas' Aunt Bee would buy some of those pretty dresses from the twins' mom for Leila. Eventually every time she made the twins an outfit she made one for Leila too. The girls were always seen walking, skipping and playing around town. Soon more and more people starting requesting dresses and the twins mom was proud as she was earning money doing something she enjoyed.

The twins never went to college but they always talked or met almost every day when Leila would get out of her college classes. Maxine got married first to a local mechanic that owned his own repair shop and Cheryl married one year later to a truck driver. Both husbands had been considered a good catch in the community. Maxine was doing well and she and Leila talked frequently until the birth of Maxines' daughter who was born with Down syndrome. Leila would visit but she noticed the spunk had drained out of Maxine. Leila believed that Maxine was sad and depressed because when she would visit Maxine would always ask about what Leila was up to but after she ask she would fade out and never seemed to be really listening.

Leila continued to visit Maxine throughout her depression stage for the next two years and at one point she seemed to get better especially when Maxine found out she was pregnant again with a son. The girls started hanging out again and Cheryl would come over to Maxines' house and the three of them would laugh and talk like they were kids again. Cheryl had taken the time to learn how to sew from her mother and she and Leila would sew cute booties and hats for the new baby. Somehow the thought of a new baby she hoped would be normal had given Maxine something to feel excited about. Leila was feeling whole again until Maxine gave birth to her son who also was born with Down syndrome. Maxine completely shut down and did not want to see any visitors including her sister Cheryl and Leila.

Cheryl and Leila did not know what to do other than just give Maxine the time she needed to get through her depression. They started to just hang out together discussing Maxine and possible ways to help her. Cheryls' life seemed quite ordinary as she was married but had not had kids yet. Her husband the truck driver was away from home a lot and always on the road. She told Leila that she had decided to go back to college and major in office technology too. Right now she was working at the local sewing factory making pillows and linens but was hungry for something different. Leila would talk to Cheryl about feeling lonely and like an outsider because she was not married and only had her aunt and empty house to come home to. Cheryl told Leila to consider herself lucky that she was free to do whatever, whenever she wanted. She told her not to rush to get married because it was not all that she had expected it to be.

Leila was still thinking about the potential husbands that she had let slip away. Some of them were professionals now and doing very well. All of them were off the market now and seemed happily married. There was Richard the store owner, Wesley the minister, Tim also a minister and Josh who now owned a car dealership. There were also some local factory and lumberyard workers who were not considered the best but still were single and available but her Aunt Bee did not and would not approve of Leila dating let alone marrying one of these men. The one that pestered her aunt the most was Gerald a local lumber yard worker who was awkward and short in stature. He was about ten years older than Leila but very boy like in manner. He had a stuttering speech problem and would constantly trip over his own feet while walking. His clumsiness seemed to get worse every time Leila would come around him. Gerald could often be found hanging out at the local restaurant lunch counter in town around noon each day. That is where he and most of the workers would go for lunch. Leila was petite, beautiful, five feet and ten inches tall with beautiful long flowing hair. Her good looks and elegant grace earned her the nickname Barbie around town. Even though Gerald was older, he looked more like her kid brother Todd, following her around instead of the tall handsome boyfriend Ken. He always offered to carry her groceries, load her bags into the car, and give her little tokens like flowers and trinkets. Leila thought he was sweet but knew that her Aunt Bee would never approve of him.

One time Gerald came by Leilas' house with flowers and offered to take her out to the movies. Aunt Bee told him to leave and never come back because Leila would never be interested in him. Later on when Leila saw him again at the market she apologized for her aunt but told him that she did not think that he should come by again. Gerald smiled and wore a goofy grin as he was not listening. He told Leila that he knew her aunt did not like him because he was not a professional man. Gerald knew that he would probably never work in a professional job because he dropped out of school in the eighth grade but enjoyed his job working at the local lumberyard. Each day Leila saw Gerald at the market and she apologized again about the way her aunt had acted. She told him again that it was best if he does not try to contact her anymore but he continued to meet and greet her every weekend at the market where he knew she would be. Every time he saw her he would not leave without giving her flowers or some little trinket to show his affection.

When Aunt Bee died in that spring she left Leila the land, house and plenty of money to pay off all of her debt from college and the loan note on her car. Suddenly Leila felt all alone again and started spending her spare time going to visit her brothers and sisters. That same year she learned that her brother Elroy had died in a car accident leaving behind a wife and four children. At the funeral Leila saw all of her sisters and brothers but it seemed that they were all close and she thought maybe it was because they had all been kept together with at least one sibling and she had been by herself. Leila wanted to help her brother Elroy's wife, Martha out anyway she could so she would sometimes pick of the children, three girls and a boy and take them to her house for the weekend. She showered them with gifts, clothes and fine food as she remembered what it felt like to lose a parent. She often asked Martha if she wanted to go but she declined and Mary believe that she just needed the time alone to grieve.

Keeping busy with her nieces and nephews on the weekends only kept Leilas mind off of the loneliness for a little while. During the week was very difficult for her to come home every day to that empty house. In town she would run into some of those old friends that used to be potential suitors. They would always ask her why she was not married by now. They would joke her saying that she would end up just like her aunt, old and alone because she had now lost out on her chance to marry. Leila believed that they were just bitter and jealous because she did not choose any of them.

However their comments did affect her because it was then, that Leila starting dating Gerald. She started believing that Gerald was the only man left that was still interested in her. This caused lots of gossip around town as people saw them as an unlikely pair. People around town believed Gerald was beneath Leila as he was poor, still struggling with his speech problem and always tripping over his own feet. He wore these big steel toe boots that were required on the lumberyard but they were too big for his foot causing him to stumble around. Leila soon met disapproval from everyone she knew, including family, friends, and even church members. Even the local town officials who knew and respected her Aunt Bee felt it necessary to tell her how disappointed they were with her choice as they had expected more from her. Leila ignored them as she felt she was happy and Gerald kept her from feeling alone.

Even after all that formal training, education and social reforming, Leila my mom succumbed to the pressure of wanting to be like the other women she knew. They were all wives and mothers that seemed happy with their husbands and children. After all that time there were no single men that came close to her approval. They simply did not measure up to her standards of what her future husband should be like. Leila knew that her standards were put in place by her aunt and had resulted in her loneliness.

Gerald allowed Leila to relax and experience some the simple things in life. He taught her to be carefree and enjoy some of life's pleasures. She lost her old self completely when she was with him and dived head first into what some thought was a hopeless future. None of it seemed to matter because within year after her aunt's death she married Gerald that summer. They were married at the courthouse which was a far stretch from the elegant church wedding she and her aunt had always dreamed of. They had a simple reception in the garden on her fathers' farm at Dowls' Plantation. Her father, Grandmother Mary and most of her brothers and sisters were there but Gerald's mother and father were the only family to attend from his side of the family. His parents did not say much but congratulations, took pictures and left after they ate. It was a very simple ceremony but somehow lacking in the usual cheer and joy most people experience or witness at weddings. Probably because many people commented that her aunt had turned over in her grave as a result of Leilas' decision. They left the reception that night and she moved him into the beautiful colonial house that her aunt left to Leila. They had no honeymoon as Gerald had no money or any concept about weddings or what should take place. The next day they went out to dinner and took in a movie together excited and happy just to be in each other's company.

After a year of marriage Gerald was happy as he was now living in a beautiful house, driving a nice car and Leila was still working at the utility company. Gerald started becoming increasing jealous. He started questioning Leila about who she talked to, what she was doing, and who she came in contact with at work. Gerald begged Leila to quit her job stating that she was married now and married women do not work. Leila knew that Gerald was just jealous of all the attention she was getting and was insecure about the fact that she had so many interested men that felt she could find someone better than him. Even after Leila expressed that she was not interested in starting a family at the moment, Gerald purposely kept trying until he succeeded in getting Leila pregnant with his first son. Gerald was happy because Leila was forced to quit as expected mothers were not popular in the workforce at that time. Three months later after Leila quit her job Gerald received a pink slip from the lumberyard and was laid off. She encouraged him to look for other employment maybe driving trucks like Cheryls' husband or working at the utility company like her brother John. Gerald refused, stating that it was only a temporary layoff. Leila did not worry too much because she still had a little savings left from the inheritance her Aunt Bee had left her and surely Gerald would be recalled back to the lumberyard in a few weeks. The lumberyard had plenty of layoffs in the past especially during the sixties but they were always able to bring most of the employees back to work. Leila felt secure as she owned her house, the car and had no other debt. Leila had one thousand dollars put away to carry them through this rough patch. Utilities, food and gas were her only bills so with careful budgeting they would be ok for at about six months.

Six months later Adam was born that summer and Leila was beginning to miss some of the luxuries to which she had become accustomed to. She now regretted that she had quit her job and had to rely on Gerald to provide for her. Leila had made more money at the utility company than Gerald did at the lumberyard so there was a shortage of income on top of more expenses because of the new baby. By the time the baby was born the thousand dollars she had saved as a cushion was almost gone. Gerald still had not been called back to work at the lumberyard. Leila breastfed as did most mothers then and she received lots of clothes from her friends at her baby shower. Cheryl was six months pregnant too with a little girl and had made some cute hats and booties hoping that their babies would grow up as friends just like they did.

Even Maxine showed up with gifts and lots of baby stuff that she thought Leila could use as she had decided that she would not be having any more children. She had come to terms with the fact that she was the mother of two children with Down syndrome and could not risk having another child that would require so much from her mentally, emotionally and physically. She loved her children but knew that her life would be different from here on out. Leila was very thrilled to see her and happy that Maxine was interacting and socializing again. She still was not the familiar comedian with a joyful laugh but a warm smile was good enough for Leila.

The baby shower helped out a lot and help saved money but it was still hard for Leila not being able to do the things she enjoyed like getting her hair done at the salon and occasionally going out for dinner at her usual fancy restaurants. All that had stopped when they got married not because of money but because Leila could not stand the looks and stares she would receive when out with Gerald. It seemed everyone she knew felt it was their duty to let her know just how disappointed they were and how much they disapproved of her husband.

The bills continued coming in with no income to pay them. Leila found out they now had to pay additional penalties as a result of paying late. She was so busy with the baby and needed Gerald's help around the house, so she asked Gerald to pay the bills she had given him. She remembered handing him the bills, telling him how much to pay and sending him downtown to pay them. Gerald had gotten them mixed up and that resulted in some being over paid and others short for the month. Leila questioned Gerald asking him how he could make such a stupid mistake. Even if he forgot what she said the balance amount was clearly written on the bill but he just shrugged his shoulders and apologized.

Not too long after Gerald kept making the same mistakes over and over, not just with the bills but now with grocery list, recipes and other instructions. She found out that Gerald could barely read. She wondered how she could have missed the signs but thinking back there was never really an opportunity outside of church that she saw him ever look at a book. Even then he always insisted that she carry and find the scriptures in the bible as they would follow along with the minister standing side by side in the church pew. When they went out he would never order off a menu, as he would just ask the waitress what was their special or ask Leila what she wanted to eat. At the courthouse Leila filled out the marriage license and even the wedding ceremony was a simple "I do". She felt that she had been misled; she knew marriage would have its trials but this was a heavy blow she was not ready to handle. How could they ever advance or do better in life if he was unable to read and get a better job. Suddenly Leilas' spirit and dream of one day getting back to her luxury life started to disappear.

Just when Leila was about to give up on Gerald ever finding a job he was called back to work at the lumberyard. It had been almost a year and things were getting rough. Leila had gone to her father for money and was getting food from the farm. Her biggest embarrassment was not having enough money to buy diapers for Adam. People were now using disposable diapers including Cheryl who would gasp at the sight of Leila having to rinse and wash Adams messy cloth diapers. Leila would have to wash and hang them out to dry every night so that he would have clean diapers the next day. Leila constantly complained to Gerald about it but he would dismiss it as he was accustomed to seeing his mother and other women washing out cloth diapers all his life. His family never had much money and they were always poor. He was accustomed to never having access to new or fancy things. He felt Leila was spoiled and just not accustomed to how other people did things during her upbringing with her aunt.

He even talked Leila into growing a garden so they could have their own food. Leila did not mind as it gave her something to do as well as provided them food so that she did not have to keep going to her fathers' farm for handouts. Even the farm workers would frown and shake their heads at the once elegant daughter they all admired every time she used to come visit her father. Her father had offered Gerald a job but Gerald swore that he would never work on a farm again. Gerald was angry at Leila for asking because he felt she was sheltered and never could relate to his hard life growing up and working on a farm.

With Gerald now back to work at the lumberyard they now were starting to get caught up on their bills. Leila was ready to be able to go back to the market to grocery shop and even though it was almost time to potty train Adam she still wanted to purchase some of those disposable diapers Cheryl was using. Just as things were looking up for her and Gerald, Leila found out that she was pregnant again. Even though she knew things would be tough and probably harder than before she was excited because this time it was a girl.

Gerald was back to work at the lumberyard for almost a year now and they seemed to be just getting by when the car broke down one afternoon on his way home from work. Gerald knew nothing about fixing cars or fixing anything else. The car was now stalling and occasionally it was slow to respond or change gears which for most men would have signaled something was wrong with the ignition starter or maybe the transmission. Leila had questioned Gerald multiple times about the problem and asked him to let Maxines husband the mechanic evaluate it at his shop. Gerald was not fond of Maxines' husband or Cheryl's husband who would sit around and talk about the automobile industry, the trucking business and sports. Gerald was not into any of those things and they were big, husky, masculine men. They would often joke Gerald because of his small statute and speech problem. They too felt that Leila was a great catch and that Gerald did not deserve to have her as his wife.

Gerald was not a handy man so any task requiring more than the basic hammer or screwdriver left him clueless. Sometimes the electrical fuse boxes would blow out and Leila would have to be the one to repair or insert new fuses. Gerald had never lived in a house with electricity and had no concept about how the electrical system worked. Gerald tried repeatedly to restart the car and when it did finally start it would not switch into the drive position so he popped the hood of the car took a look and browsed around to see if he spotted anything loose or smoking. Gerald realized that he did not know what to do so he locked the car and started the two mile walk home from the lumberyard.

When he arrived home and told Leila about what happened with the car she was very upset and started asking Gerald why he did not take the car to Maxine's husband as she had asked. He simply shrugged his shoulders and went into the kitchen and washed his hands for dinner. She was so frustrated because she believed Gerald never took any matter serious. She sometimes felt as if he was another child that she had to constantly care for and check up on. She desperately wanted him to be the kind of husband who could lead and take charge of things without being told. That night the stress from Gerald and the car situation caused Leila to have contractions and she went into labor. Leila called the ambulance as they did not have a car to drive to the hospital. Gerald took Adam over to the neighbors while he rode in the ambulance with Leila to the hospital. Leila felt this childbirth and delivery was very different from what she experienced with Adam. Adam's childbirth was quick, fast and easy but Leila was beginning to believe rumors that girls were always harder than boys in childbirth. After twelve hours of what Leila believed was the worst experience, she gave birth to Lisa, her new baby girl.

After Lisa was born Leila was very happy because secretly she had been wishing and hoping for a girl since her pregnancy with Adam. Gerald was very proud and held Lisa for hours regardless of her crying or fussiness. When visitors would come to visit he would stand and watch over them as to make sure they did not harm his precious baby girl. Cheryl and Maxine came by to visit and Leila took the opportunity to ask Maxine if her husband could take a look at their car which had been broken down for a week now. Maxine was feeling sorry for Leila. She talked to her husband and begged him to fix the car so that it would reduce some of the stress on Leila. She had mentioned that Gerald had not said anything to her husband about fixing the car and Leila was upset as she felt that it should have been his top priority as a husband and now a father of two.

Lisa's Journey

From that moment on Lisa came to be known as Leila and Gerald's only little girl. After Lisa they gave birth to her little brother Elijah almost exactly one year later. Leila was very embarrassed by that pregnancy as everyone knew about their hardship and struggle. They could not believe that she was pregnant again not even three months after Lisa's birth. At this time Adam was now four years old, Lisa was one and Elijah was a newborn. Leila had three very small children at home to care for and was sad, lonely and depressed. Her daily schedule consisted of breastfeeding, changing diapers and washing clothes. Leila and Gerald also had to apply for public assistance. They were receiving food stamps, Medicaid and WIC. Leila was still very proud and refused to stand in line for the free food program that is until things got really hard and money really tight. Gerald was reduced to part time at the lumberyard so Leila put her pride aside because she could not bear to go back to her father for assistance.

Lisa was about three years old so Leila and Gerald would take her to stand in line for free food handouts every month. The organization sponsoring the food drive was located in the next town over and it was about a twenty minute ride to get to the facility. Lisa would hear her parents talking about what they would get or ask for this time and who would take what child with them. Leila took Lisa and Elijah to stand in line with her and Gerald took Adam with him. That was their way to receive two handouts. Leila was always embarrassed when someone recognized her. She sometimes saw some of her classmates and knew that they were staring at her because she had been very popular and envied by others in her school.

Things got significantly worse over the years and Gerald was laid off again during the early 1980's. It was the technology era and more factories, lumberyards and business were replacing employees with computers. Gerald was displaced during this new movement as he was not educated as a result of dropping out of school. It was difficult for him get a new job let alone fill out an employment application.

Leila lost all her joy and passion for life because she stopped smiling and never seem to enjoy anything. She was always angry and crying about how her life was miserable and meaningless. She was no longer a size six as she had been before having children and now she was much bigger. She could not afford to buy new clothes so she was still wearing maternity clothes and hand-me downs other people had given her while she was pregnant.

Leilas' daily routine consisted of waking up, cooking breakfast and going to the post office. Her morning trip to the post office was a way for her to get out of the house. When she got home Leila would start on lunch and then sit down and watch television all day only stopping long enough to clean up a mess or change a diaper. She would have a daily sitcom schedule and always manage to cook, clean and have dinner on the table when Gerald came home.

When all the children started school Leila became lonelier at home but enjoyed her break at the same time. It was sort of bittersweet. She would always walk them to the bus stop in the morning, kiss them goodbye and be there to pick them up every afternoon with a hug. She actually had a little bit of freedom now because the oldest son Adam was in the third grade, Lisa in the first grade and Elijah was starting kindergarten in the fall. Things were starting to get better for Leila for about two years until the unexpected happened. This may have been the breaking point for Leila when she became pregnant again with another son, Gavin. All of the new found freedom Leila was use to having would now disappear.

Over the years Leila's physical and mental health continued to digress through the years and she was diagnosed with depression. During this phase she no longer cared for herself, Gerald or the children. When Leila was healthy she would make sure the children had neatly pressed clothes and Lisa had colorful barrettes in her hair just to go for a walk in the park or playground.

When Lisa was in the first grade she wanted to wear her hair out in a big hair style and curls. Lisa thought that look was cool and she had previously argued with Leila because she always put her hair in ponytails and barrettes. Even though Lisa was only in elementary school she wanted to look like the high school girls that she saw at the bus stop in the mornings. After a while Leila stop doing Lisa's hair but Lisa never complained because she hated the Sunday night three hour ritual of washing, conditioning, blow drying, and then braiding her hair. Lisa saw it as her moment to be able to do her own thing with her hair and soon everyone at school including her teachers noticed that there was a change in her hair and appearance. Not only was she styling her own hair at six but she was also picking her own clothes. Sometimes Lisa did not have the best fashion sense because often she ignored style, weather conditions and seasons of the year. Maybe it was the flip flops and cute t-shirt she wore under her coat that raised suspension that she may not have had anyone watching over her.

Lisa remembered shortly after the holidays being called in to the counselor's office and being asked about how things were going at home with her mom and dad. They asked her if she had food, where she slept and if anyone was hitting her. She replied that everything was ok but she was nervous because she was not sure if her brothers answered all their questions as confidently as she did. Shortly after that her family received a visit from a social worker. She came into their home and looked in all the rooms, refrigerator, closets and bathrooms.

Ironically the pipes had frozen and burst underneath the house so Gerald turned off all the water because it was leaking below the house. He did not want to risk anymore foundation problems. The kitchen sink was leaning because the leaking pipes had rotted the floor. Gerald would only run water through the bathroom. That was not a major deal because if they were thirsty Leila would just fill a pitcher of water up and put it in the refrigerator. If she needed water to cook or wash dishes she would keep a large wash bucket of water on the table in the kitchen. The social worker was a young woman from up north and obviously had no idea that everyone down south did not live in pristine conditions. She documented everything and news in a small town travels fast. From that point on the whole family was under the radar at school and in the community.

Everywhere they went people were asking questions all the time. News even got out to some of Leila's friends and relatives who came by to check on her. Leila was changing because she was not going out to visit her friends, neighbors and even missing church. She withdrew and isolated herself from everyone that loved her and eventually she was diagnosed with severe depression and then a mental illness. Leila lost her battle and after witnessing what happened to her mother, Lisa vowed that she would never give up or give in to life's struggles and challenges.

Lisa found her escape through school and then college where she quickly met her husband Jacob. She dated him throughout her freshman year of college and with all the freedom from home she became pregnant with her son. Lisa and Jacob were quickly married and they moved into a small one bedroom house that ended up being anything but a happy home. With the stress of being parents, and bills they realized that neither one of them was happy with the other. The arguing and then fighting seemed like it went on and on forever until one day Lisa realized one of them needed to leave before they killed each other. They were angry, unhappy and bitter with how their lives turned out and Lisa refused to follow in her mom's footsteps.

Lisa appreciated his sacrifice of dropping out of college and taking a job in an electronics store to pay the bills and take care of them but she still could not excuse his resentment and evil disposition toward her. While he worked, she decided to go back to school taking classes whenever she could during the evening, online, and even during the summer with the help of friends and family. Lisa was so zealous in the pursuit of her college education that she finished school on time and with a double major. She knew that it was her ticket out and she had to stay and do whatever it took until she graduated.

Through the years their communication and relationship with one another got worse. The yelling turned into physical fighting and the police were called to the house several times by concerned neighbors. Lisa now only had one semester left of college and it seemed like things were getting worse every day. She knew that things were getting bad when she started sleeping with a knife under her pillow. She tried spending as much time as possible away from the house just so they would not fight.

Lisa was trying to stay busy to make the little time she had left go by as fast as possible. While her son was in daycare she became very active on campus and joined as many clubs as possible. She held officer positions, was very social, made good grades and she was well liked by her classmates and professors. Lisa was even nominated by two of her clubs for the title of Miss Business and Miss Marketing on the university royal court. She felt like Cinderella during the coronation ball and dreaded going back home to the reality of her life.

Jacob was very jealous and made it very difficult for Lisa to be happy and actively participate or interact with others on campus. He even decreased his work hours to part time status and enrolled back into classes at the university just so he could monitor and watch everything Lisa was doing on campus. Jacob was further along in his engineering degree program than Lisa and decided to finish taking his last couple of classes so that he could graduate first.

Lisa had now been accepted into the best and most elite sorority on campus. Delta Kappa Lambda was known for their scrutiny and difficult selection process. Out of two hundred young ladies that applied for membership, Lisa was one of only seven young ladies selected for membership that year. It was very hard work to keep her personal life a secret but she managed to keep the sorority intrigued with all of the positive things she was doing on campus.

Jacob hated the sorority and did everything possible to prevent Lisa from being able to socialize with her sisters. Lisa had become really close with her new sisters and they started spending more time together. One of them was Becky, the daughter of Jacobs' boss and she was also the niece of one of his favorite professors so it was hard for him to show his true colors when Becky would come over to visit Lisa. Lisa knew that she had to use the friendship to her advantage so she kept inviting Becky over as often as possible to prevent the usual arguing and fighting that went on at home.

Everything was fine for a while until Jacob graduated that semester. He quit his part time job at the electronics store and he no longer needed to impress Becky so Lisa became distant from her from fear of her learning her secret. Jacob also took the keys to the car and stop giving Lisa money so she could not go anywhere. Things were going well for him as he landed a great job downtown in the mayors' office as a community development engineer. He was now socializing and mingling with all of the community leaders, police and anyone else that shared a space in the municipal building. Lisa could not believe the transformation he went through every day when he left home. It was like watching Dr. Jekyll and Mr. Hyde as he interacted and laughed with two of his new friends' downtown. She recognized one of them as the major from the campaign signs around town but she did not know who the other man was.

Things got bad again and one night Jacob and Lisa starting fighting again. They starting hitting and throwing things at each other, then Jacob started choking Lisa while she was at the top of the stairs. Lisa was trying so hard to get away that she fell down the stairs and landed on her face. One of the neighbors had already called the police again and they busted through the door when they heard the screams. Lisa lost consciousness for a few seconds and when she opened her eyes she was lying there at the bottom of the steps hurt, bruised and barely conscious. Somehow Jacob was now standing over her at the bottom of the stairs explaining to the police what happened. As the officers lifted her up off the floor they asked if she was ok. Lisa stated that she was ok because she did not feel as though she broke any bones. The officers asked if they had been fighting and Lisa said yes. They told her that because they both had injuries then they would have to arrest both of them for domestic violence and her son would go to foster care unless she had someone to pick him up. Lisa was very afraid of social services and fear of not getting her son back if they got involved. Both Jacob and Lisa's parents were over two hours away and she had not talked to her brothers in months. The only thing she knew to do was call Becky. Becky came right over to watch her son before they even left for the police station.

Lisa knew that her secret was out and finally everyone would know about her life. As she sat on that bench in the police station waiting to talk to the magistrate she decided that she would tell everything. It seemed like hours had passed by and finally they called her name to tell her recollection of the events. When she appeared before the magistrate she knew that she had recognized him from somewhere but at first she could not pinpoint where. It was only when she told her story and he laughed at her did she remember that he was the other man she saw having lunch with Jacob. He told her that Jacob had appeared before him first and told his story. He stated that he believed that she was the cause of the entire situation. He said that he knew Jacob personally and believed he could never do the things she said he did.

He told her that he would not apply a bond for her if they both agreed to stay away from each other. He said that he had ordered a restraining order against her on behalf of Jacob. Lisa could not believe what she was hearing but knew that there was nothing she could do about it because he and Jacob were good friends. She asked the magistrate if she could place a restraining order on him as well and he said yes but Jacob used the home address as his place of residence so she would have to list another address. Lisa then asked about her son and the magistrate said that neither of them had a custody order so he could not prohibit either one of them from getting her son. Lisa was so happy that she had left her son with Becky where he was safe and far away from Jacob.

Lisa told the magistrate that she did not have a place to go as her family was two hours away and she now had no access to a car. He told her that surely she could find someone who would take her home to her parents' house or he could have her dropped off at a women's shelter. Lisa knew she was not considering going home as an option because she only had four months left in school and she was not about to let Jacob ruin her future. She knew Becky and the rest of her sorority sisters lived on campus in the dorm and she could not stay there, so she agreed that she would go to the shelter.

Lisa made a phone call to Becky to check on her son. She finally told Becky everything that had been going on between her and Jacob and apologized for being embarrassed about telling her. Becky was crying more than Lisa and said that she had suspected it the entire time and she was sorry she never said or did anything to help. She asked Lisa if there was anything she could do and said that she had already called all of the sorority sisters together for a meeting.

When Lisa finally signed all of her papers it was almost morning. When she walked out of the police station she saw her sorority sisters standing there waiting for her. They were so comforting and promised to help her anyway they could during the entire ride back to the sorority house. Lisa was barely listening as all she could think about was seeing her son. When she got there he was still asleep and she suddenly felt calmer. She still could not believe the ordeal that she had just been through.

Lisa spent the next couple of days in the sorority house until the weekend came and she knew she had to go to the shelter. Gossip had spread and even her old friends from back home came by to help her. Lisa was not happy with her situation but she had to make the best of it if she was going to make it to graduation. They brought her clothes, food and a small heater because they knew Lisa was anemic and always cold. She was only allowed to go back to her house once to pick up her personal belongings while an officer was present. Even though she recognized this particular officer as another one of Jacobs' friends he was nice enough to let her pick up a few things for her son too.

The women's shelter was not as bad as she thought. It was an older Victorian home that a previous victim had donated as a gift after she became successful. They provided her with the biggest bedroom because of her son, free food, brand new clothes, and transportation back and forth to the university as well as to the daycare. Lisa promised that she would give back to the shelter one day as she was very thankful for the opportunity they were giving her.

During all of her turmoil, Lisa had managed to be nominated for a business internship position with one of the top financial companies located on Wall Street in New York. Her professors had thought so highly of her and their recommendation was placed before the incidence with Jacob had taken place. Lisa was grateful for the opportunity and decided to put all of her effort into impressing the judges in her upcoming interview.

On the day of her interview, Lisa felt like she had wowed the judges with all of her accomplishments and academic success but she was not prepared for the questions they asked concerning her personal life. It seemed that someone had told them that she was a young mother and they wanted to know what resources or plans she had in place to be able to fulfill the internship total hour requirement if she was awarded the position.

Lisa had not even thought that far ahead but she remembered that her mother had two sisters and lots of aunts, uncles and cousins she heard that lived there. Even though she had not spoken with them since her high school graduation she knew that at least one of them would be willing to let her and her son live with them. Lisa proudly and confidently informed them that her personal life would not have a negative effect on her position if awarded and her responsibilities would make her work harder and value the opportunity more than her competitors.

Lisa was so nervous when she walked out of the interview as she felt the fate of her entire life rested on the decision they were about to make. It would be another month before she would hear the results of the internship selection process. Lisa was so excited that she decided to go the daycare early to pick up her son so he could play in the park before they went back to the shelter. She always tried to tire him out so that he would be sleepy when they got there and not disturb the other shelter residents. Even though she was grateful for the assistance Lisa felt like she was always under such watchful eyes because she was the youngest mother living there and they were monitoring everything she did.

When Lisa got to the shelter they told her that his father already picked him up. They had told her a few minutes before that he had stopped by to visit with him but he only stayed a few times and Lisa was not worried because even though they could not get along he would never hurt their son. This time was obviously different and Lisa panicked as she knew that he was not just spending time with him. Somehow she knew that he would not be bringing him back. Jacob had been calling her saying that they should forgive each other and get back together. Lisa would just ignore him as she knew he could not come near her because of the protective order.

When she called the police they said it was nothing she could do because he was legally his father too and there was no custody order in place. At first he took him to his mothers but when Lisa showed up there he enrolled him in a new day care center with a false name just to keep her from finding them. After Lisa visited what seem like every daycare center in the world she found him playing outside of this little house with a white picket fence. When Lisa saw her son he got excited and started laughing with joy. The daycare provider came out and Lisa identified herself and told her that she was taking him with her. The daycare provider said that she could not allow that and she called Jacob and the police. Lisa told her that she was not trying to cause her problems and she would wait there with her until they arrived. When the officers arrived her son was sitting on her lap and hugging her tightly. She told them the situation and showed them her identification. When Jacob arrived they asked him if Lisa was the mother and he said yes. Then they told him that she had got there first and whoever the son was with at the moment had temporary custody since no court order was in place.

Lisa took her son back to the shelter as quick as she could and all night she thought about how close she was to graduation. She wondered how she was going to be able to finish school these last couple of months and Jacob was also calling and pleading with her to come back. She thought about how sweet he was whenever they would make up and all she needed to do was keep things calm enough for the next couple of months so that she could finish her degree. Lisa was stuck. She knew what he wanted and she would not be able to keep her son away from him and go to class too. It was that next day that Lisa decided to put her happiness aside and do what she had to do.

The next couple of months were like walking on eggshells for Lisa trying to keep things calm and perfect at home. The people at the shelter thought she was making a big mistake but kept the door opened for her if she wanted to come back. Becky disagreed with her decision but supported her as well. Two months later Lisa walked across that stage and afterwards she packed her bags, left Jacob and walked out the door.

After graduation, Lisa decided to move in with her aunt who lived in New Jersey. It was a tough decision on who she would live with because she had several options considering two of her mom's sisters lived there along with four great aunts all eager to help her reach the goals her mom did not. She landed a junior accountant job with a nonprofit accounting firm in Manhattan, New York. Lisa had it all figured out. Her aunt was on disability and volunteered to watch her son while she worked. She got her commute schedule down to forty-five minutes by taking a fifteen minute bus ride into Newark pen station and then a twenty minute train into the world trade center followed by a three block walk over to Wall Street.

Lisa could not believe it at first. She was actually living her dream, wearing the power suit, stepping long and strong with all of the other business executives. Lisa could not stop smiling as she looked down at her new leather briefcase. The first task they gave her was actually auditing the financial records of a woman's shelter. She visited other various nonprofit corporations throughout the city making sure they were financially sound and in compliance with the law. Lisa enjoyed it a lot and made lots of new friends. The money was good however she rarely saw her son because of the long hours at work. Everything was going so smoothly until September 11, 2001. Her daily commute usually took over an hour but when the World Trade Center went down and the accounting firm suffered emotionally due to the loss of some of their employees. Eventually the owner decided to relocate the business and Lisa decided that it would be too much of a commute for her. Eventually she moved back to South Carolina where her old professor had offered her a job teaching business. Lisa took the position and decided to pursue her master's degree while waiting for a position at one of the local accounting firms.

She was able to buy a new car and her very first house. The house was truly a dream come true for Lisa because it was a beautiful brick three bedroom home with a two car garage, vaulted ceilings, full room over the garage for an office, fenced in back yard for her son to play and a sunroom for her. The owner was an older lady who lived by herself and the house was purchased for her by her son who was in the military. Every where the son went, he moved his mother with him and purchased her a home then he would sell it when he was assigned to new duty station. The home was located in one of the newest subdivisions in the city. It was actually the best home in the neighborhood and was only five years old. Lisa purchased her dream home for one hundred and fifty thousand dollars and she did not know that in the four years that she lived there they built six more subdivisions directly around her house. The builders decided to save money on the newest phases of homes by going with a more basic "cookie cutter" design therefore causing the value of Lisa's home to nearly double because of all the extra features it had inside.

When Lisa had her home appraised she nearly fainted when the appraiser told her it was valued at two hundred and fifty thousand dollars. Her realtor suggested she ask for two hundred and seventy five dollars so that she would have a little extra left over. At that moment in her life she knew that her life was about to change. After she accepted an offer on the house she started making preparations to move. Lisa spent many hours thinking and planning what her new life would be like with that much money. She was already dreaming of her new house, luxury car and all of the nice things she would buy her son and her family.

Her fantasy suddenly ended when her realtor called. The realtor and the lawyer were together on a conference call. They told her that since she purchased the house while she was still married, according to South Carolina state law, she would have to have her soon to be ex-husband's signature in order to sell it. Lisa was upset and did not know what to do because her divorce would not be final for another three months. Lisa's relationship with Jacob was not good and she knew the situation would take some finesse considering how they ended things when she walked out on him after her graduation. She eventually called and asked him if he would sign the papers. At first he said no but then he asked for money. Lisa never told him how much money she was receiving for the house so when he asked for ten thousand dollars she quickly agreed.

A week later, Jacob requested twenty thousand and then changed it to fifty thousand dollars a couple of days later. Lisa refused and he got mad and stated that he had seen the home listed online. Jacob knew how much Lisa was getting so on the week of the closing he demanded half of the profit or he would not sign the closing documents. Lisa thought about how she had already packed the house. She had already purchased another home, resigned from her old job and accepted a new position in a new city. She was ready to move and eager for a fresh start so after hours of yelling and screaming she agreed because she knew that she could not miss this opportunity for a new beginning. Lisa thought about her son and realized just how many people were counting on her.

On the day of closing Lisa showed up at the law office with the biggest smile but it quickly faded as she sat there waiting for Jacob to arrive and sign. She must have called and texted him over a hundred times. Lisa did not get a response, so she called his job and asked them if they could try reaching him for her. Lisa will never forget the sound of his voice when Jacob finally called her back. She could not even understand him because he was so busy laughing hysterically. Jacob stopped laughing and with the calmest voice he said, "Did you really think I was going to help you get rich after everything I did for you. Forget the money, I don't even want it. Seeing you suffer is worth more than gold," and then he hung up. After the initial shock, Lisa realized what had just happened. All she could do was cry, right there in front of her realtor, lawyer and the couple that wanted to buy her house. After Lisa excused herself and went outside her realtor and lawyer came out to check on her. She told them what Jacob said and even though they felt sympathy for her they explained that there was nothing they could do because Lisa had to have his signature. On top of all of her financial loss she would also have to reimburse the unsuspecting couple who had already moved out of their home and had nowhere to live now.

It was then that Lisa decided that she hated Jacob more than ever and would never forgive him for what he did. About a week went by and she decided that she would have to make a choice. Would she stay or would she go. The new house was in another city about thirty miles away. She realized that her plan was still in place and even though she would not be receiving the money that she had dreamed about, she still had a chance to start over again. Lisa decided to let it all go, move away and leave everything behind. She chose to let the house go into foreclosure and luckily she had a little savings still left over so she decided to move and embrace this new season and transition in her life.

After Lisa moved about one hundred miles away to a new city, Jacob went to the court and filed for sole custody of their son. Jacob told Lisa that she could not erase him out of their son's life. Lisa said that she was not trying to keep him from their son but she only wanted a healthy distance between them.

Finally they agreed on joint custody. Lisa would have her son during the week and Jacob would get visitation every weekend. They would meet in a nearby city that served as the half way point between their two cities. It worked for a little while until one day Lisa called to let Jacob know that she was running late and he told her it was no problem because he was already in her town. She later found out that weekend when she picked her son up on Sunday that he had also moved to her town. He even leased a townhome right down the street from Lisa house. Lisa was so upset that Jacob would not respect the distance that she required between them. She was not comfortable seeing him every time she wanted to go to the grocery store, gas station or shopping. Lisa decided that day that she was going to move again. She quickly started applying for jobs in another city over about another fifty miles further away from Jacob. Within two weeks Lisa received an offer for a new position and within one month she moved again. She was not happy about the fact that she had to uproot her son again who was finally starting to like his new home and school but Lisa new that she could not be anywhere near Jacob in order to be happy and have peace. She hoped that this time Jacob would finally get the point that she did not want to reconcile or be near him.

Recognizing Your Season

Lisa was not always able to recognize her season and sometimes she had trouble keeping her faith and pressing through life's trials and tribulations. Lisa moved to another city thinking that would solve her problems. She ran away from her problems and wanted to start a new life. She quickly found out that a new place just meant new people and new problems. She was dealing with a divorce, sexual harassment at work, tax, credit problems, a custody battle and issues with child support. After a long hard custody battle with her ex husband and thousands of dollars later, they agreed on joint custody. Lisa would have her son Monday through Friday and he would have him every weekend and the entire summer. At first she was angry because she had left everything else behind and felt that he was using the one thing that he knew would hurt her and that was taking her son away from her. By the summer Lisa began to finally accept the custody arrangement and then she just buried herself into more work.

It was then that she met her knight in shining armor Ben, a very prominent and wealthy man. She thought he was an angel because he was so nice, kind and willing to give her everything that her heart desired. Lisa began spending her weekends with him and soon she became attached to him. He was accepting of her past and her son but he was in the military and she found herself getting very attached to him. He had never been married and did not have any children. Lisa refused to let him help her financially but she depended on him emotionally. After two years of what she thought was a wonderful relationship, he told her that he was getting a promotion and his duty station changed and was being reassigned out of the state. Ben asked her if she wanted him to stay. Lisa said yes but she did not want him to regret and resent her later if he did not take this opportunity. Ben left. Lisa was full of sadness and started isolating herself because she missed him so much.

Lisa buried herself in work and tried to escape from her disappointment and sorrow. She was spending everyday hoping and wishing that he would come back. In order to help herself through all of her pain and hurt, she started a blog where people could connect and talk about their life's experiences. She felt then that although she was very young she still had been through many hardships in life that many people her age had not experienced. Lisa found herself constantly mentoring other women about life, family, career marriage, and divorce.

Talking through her blog was both uplifting and inspirational. She worked so hard day and night developing what she thought would be an inspiration to women everywhere. All her time and focus went into the blog until the day she met Edward. She felt that he was so interesting and exciting. It did not take long until he was able to take all of her attention and concentration away from her blog. She met him at the grocery store while she was getting ready for her new year's party. He was a police officer during the day and a jazz musician at night. Lisa spent the next two years mesmerized and captivated by his music and spirit. Their birthdays were only a few days apart and she felt like she had met her soul mate. They were so in tuned with each other because they both like the same things, places and music. Lisa spent all her weekends dressed up in the finest clothes watching him perform and then afterwards they would snuggle up on the couch in front of the fire place. He was very romantic, always cooking for her, lighting candles and serenading her on his guitar in front of the fire place.

He made her feel so loved and special and it was hard for her to resist his charm.

The only problem with Edward was that he was fifteen years older than Lisa and by the time she found out she was already in love with him. He did not look his age. His mind, body and spirit were very youthful. Eventually Edward's insecurity began to show and he started to question everything Lisa said and did. At first he was proud of all of the attention Lisa got from men. He loved the way she looked, dressed and acted but that soon changed. Then one day after many arguments and what felt like an interrogation session she found herself exhausted from trying to please him. Lisa stopped doing the things she loved, stopped seeing people that she enjoyed spending time with all because she wanted to please him. When the trust started to leave Lisa noticed his attention diverted away from her and more focused toward other things and places. Edward was always meeting new people and women were always all over him when he performed. She believed that the stress of their age difference magnified all the other issues in their relationship so they started spending more and more time apart. Lisa still had her weekends free but Edward stopped taking her with him to his concerts. She ignored all of the signs that something was wrong because she loved him so much and was so afraid to lose him in her life. Lisa started settling for the little time that she could get with him and eventually became lonely, emotional and codependent all over again.

Whenever Lisa got upset she just worked more. She decided she would finally follow her dream and open up her own store. She started putting all of her time and energy into her new dream. She had always loved shopping and fashion. She met a man that was making lots of money by attending auctions for abandoned storage units. He told Lisa how he would only have to bid a little money on these storage units then turn around and resale them on his website. Lisa visited his warehouse which was filled with both new and used inventory. He had everything from clothes, furniture, appliances and more. Lisa inquired what he was going to do with the entire inventory and he said that he wanted to open up a store but he did not have the time to manage it. He told Lisa that he was a single father and his trucking business was his main source of income. Lisa was stunned as she felt this was the perfect opportunity for her. She could partner with him by purchasing more inventory and running the store while he continued driving his trucks and picking up inventory. They decided to go into business together and in the beginning things were working well. That is until she found out that her partner was smuggling illegal immigrants and arranging the pick-up and delivery of mail order brides. Lisa would have never believed it until one day she overheard one of his conversation. She immediately severed ties with her partner, packed up her belongings and removed her share of the inventory and fixtures from the store. In retaliation against Lisa, her partner filed false charges of burglary against her. She found herself in the midst of more hardship and it took her many months and lots of money to sort out that mess but she quickly found out that some people you meet in life are not always what they seem to be. Lisa called Edward and with his help she was able to get the charges dropped and put that ordeal behind her.

There were so many things going on in Lisa's life during that time, so eventually it started to affect her health. It seemed like one bad thing after the next was happening. Lisa got so depressed and started isolating herself again.

One day Lisa's friend Becky called and told her that she had some unresolved issues from her childhood and marriage that were negatively affecting her life and future. Becky believed that Lisa needed to see a therapist and pray. One Wednesday night after work and running errands she was driving on her way home and she saw a billboard sign for Bible classes. When she looked behind the sign there were trees and behind it was a church. Lisa never knew why she never saw this church before until that night but she decided to go. Lisa enjoyed Bible study every week and even attended church on Sunday where she learned a lot from the pastor. One of the most powerful messages she received from him was that a message from God will always be echoed. He said that she needed to release everything inside of her and that through her story others would be uplifted and helped. She heard the same message several weeks later while visiting back home in Conboard for Mothers Day church service.

Every month the church celebrated birthdays by having all those with a birthday in that month stand up and be recognized. They made everyone line up in front of the altar to sing happy birthday. It was very uncomfortable for Lisa because some of those people she had not seen in years. The pastor came down and reached until his bag and presented her with a gift. There were lots of gifts in the bag but when he got to her he pulled out a pen. Lisa could not believe that this was the gift that he had chosen for her. It was enclosed in a plastic case with a picture of a man molding a piece of pottery with a cross on it out of clay. The phrase, *Shaped to Serve* and the scripture Isaiah 64:8 was written on it. The pastor said that she was God's handiwork, formed by him for a life of love and service now she needed to use the pen to write. Lisa knew this was the echo and almost fainted on the spot. After that she went back to her city and continued going to church and wrote down everything that stirred an emotion or memory within her.

Lisa thought about everything that was going on and when she started the blog and she did not know half of what she knew now. She knew she had powerful and soul stirring life lessons and experiences to write about. Lots of time had passed since the creation of her blog but now she was able to go back to her blog with confidence. Lisa was able to let go of all that emotional baggage and move past the hurt from her relationship with Edward.

Lisa continued to attend church and started writing notes about the messages every Sunday in church. The pastor was a very powerful messenger but it was one very enlightening message that changed Lisa's life forever. The message was titled *"The Wind is Blowing"* and it was like the pastor was looking right through her soul.

He said that the spirit of the Lord is always moving and wind is always blowing. The house of the Lord is a shelter and when a righteous man runs in then he is safe. God is constantly calling for you to seek him out because he is constantly on the move. God moved upon many prophets in the bible and then disappeared for four hundred years. Then he showed back up through miraculous conception in Mary's wound. He said that people should not fellowship with people who have empty wounds with nothing inside of them because they will drain you by pulling the life out of you. God's people are always ready for the next move. Position yourself and prepare yourself by operating from a position of strength rather than weakness.

Once the men and women of God get on one accord, there is nothing you can't accomplish no matter how small. Think and act like the ant and the locust. Ants work diligently all summer and fall storing up food for the winter. The locust learns to wait for the perfect wind and travels in ranks and bands. Follow their actions because if the people can just get on one accord, they can perform and fly like the locust.

The devil likes to go in your closet and in your past and pull out stuff against you but you have to repent, and learn how to run with hungry people. Hungry people are those people in your life that have a great appetite for God, his Word and life. You can't run with laid back, satisfied people because they will kill your hunger and your drive. Two hungry saints can turn the whole house, system, or organization around. Once you get substance in your life you can now consciously wait on the next move of God by learning to let somebody help you. Remember God will always send somebody to help you and it maybe more than one person, maybe a series of people he has aligned with purpose on your life.

The first wave or person may come into your life and die out so that the second wave or person can come in. We have to learn to press our way through life. Sometimes we get discouraged if we go knocking on doors and they do not open for us. If you can't get through the door, come in through the window. If the window is closed, then go through the gutters, over, under, through whatever way we need to but learn to press your way through life. God has ordained a plan in your life this year and even on this day. Be relentless because if it is part of God's plan they are either give it to you now or they will have to give it to you later. Just remember it is yours and you have got to claim it. The enemy thought he had you because he is constantly looking at your wings and weaknesses. They are constantly trying to find a way to clip your wings but through God you can propel yourself out and into success because timing is everything.

The locust knows how to wait for the right time when the wind is blowing and rustling then he jumps. The wind carries him for miles because he caught the right wind at the right time. The wind represents the Holy Ghost. You never know where the locust is coming from or where it is going. You just have to leap out on faith and into the anointed. When the locust leaps up into the wind it cannot navigate on its own. You cannot fly against the wind and sometimes life is hard and it is a struggle. You cannot chart your own course so wherever the wind blows is where the locust goes. Stop trying to line up things and wait until the time feels right because sometimes it is never going to feel right.

The next wind that comes by will blow you completely out of the situation. You resist because it is unfamiliar and you must be willing to go where God sends you. When the locust leaps with the wind he travels without stress because of the power of the wind. God has a place of distinction already prepared for you. For everything there is a purpose, a season and a time. You cannot teach timing because timing is something you have got to sense. You do not think about it, you just do it.

This is why the enemy sends sin into your life to dull your sense of timing. The devil cannot stop your purpose, he cannot mess with your season but he can mess with your timing. When you hear the wind blow, you have to lock down in your mind that you will not miss it this time around. Do not have a spirit like Saul. Saul tried to kill David because he was bitter that he missed his timing. Learn to pay attention and listen for your time and have the wisdom to know when to jump. You need to study the wisdom of the locust.

The locust has the wisdom to know when to jump. There are ways that seem right to man but those ways and methods can lead to destruction. The devil cannot take your peace and there is no way for him to get it unless you give it to him. We feel we have to correct it, we feel we have to fix it. It is not your job to fix it but it is your job to follow. God will come on the scene and He will make what is crooked straight again. In families and relationships, sometimes that person may not be right and all seems lost but stay positive and you can win them over. Study to keep your mouth closed and let God fight your battles for you. Stop worrying because people that worry the most feel that they are least protected.

We often lack perspective in life and lose sight of what is important. Workaholics often give all you have got to the job and have nothing left over for life and love ones. Your love ones need conversation and words too. It is often said that intellectual people lack common sense but I believe that it is not common sense they are lacking rather they lack perspective because they are so tired up with other things.

We want to pick and choose what we want to do even after God speaks to us and tells us what to do. You are destroying yourself because you are not applying the word of God that has been illuminated for you. Be anxious for nothing but for everything give prayer and supplication with thanksgiving. Make your request known to God and the peace of God which passes all understanding shall keep your hearts and minds through Jesus Christ. I repeat, do not be anxious and He will guard your heart and your mind.

Persecution Will Always Bring Direction

The pastor also used the story of how the apostles were persecuted after Jesus death. It was illegal to be a Christian and speak about Jesus. The apostles had to meet secretly underground and this went on for years because they had no place or building in which they could freely worship. We need to fully understand the price that was paid for the gospel we hear today. When we do not understand the price that was paid for us, we tend to take things for granted.

The apostles had a great deal of pressure upon them to walk with Jesus but the real pressure was after Jesus was gone and the disciples were on their own. They had to continue meeting in secrecy because all types of militia were out to kill them and all other Christians by order of Saul of Tarsus. Saul was a powerful man both brutal and ruthless who grew up hating Christians. He believed that he was doing God a favor by stumping out all Christians. The apostles simply wanted to reason with him because Saul was also a very intelligent man who could talk and persuade like no other. He spoke several different languages and was respected by all. People listened to him including royalty and militia. Surely the apostle believed that if any man could help them then it would be Saul. Unfortunately, Saul continued to persecute the apostles and he was on his way the city of Damascus with a decree in hand to annihilate all Christians including men, women and children.

The apostles were met with even more persecution and the possibility of death. The pastor quoted the scripture Romans 5:3 and said that tribulation brings patience, patience brings experience and experience brings hope and direction. God wanted them to appreciate their enemies and praise him in their hard times because it is your enemies that push you into your purpose.

It was while Saul was on his way with the decree in hand that he looked up toward the heavens and then a blinding light from the sky took away his sight. Now the famous leader of all armies now had to depend on others to lead him. Then one day Saul had a dream that a man named Ananias would come to him one day and lay hands on him. Acts 9:10-20. Ananias was sent to give Saul his sight back from God. When Saul was confronted by the man of god he had no choice but to believe. God had blinded Saul's natural eyes in order to open his spiritual eyes. God has a way of bringing your enemies down in order to humble them. Now Saul could use that same power and influence for God's work. God closed the eyes of Saul in order to reopen them for his work.

Now What Have You Learned Through Your Journey?

The story of your life is like a computer. God can wipe out everything in your life that you were once exposed to in the blink of an eye. He can fix any problem, delete your hard drive and erase all those old backed up files including memories, people and habits. He can make all that hurt, pain and sorrow go away. He is God all by himself and He does not need help from anybody to bless you but when He does get ready to bless you nobody can stop you.

When Lisa started journaling she learned that everything she went through was for a purpose and everything that came her way was ordered. She realized she had reached a place where she was content with the situations and events that transpired in her life. She thanked God for her day and her daily bread. Everything did not happen in one day so she knew she could not fix it all in one day.

As Lisa walked with God she learned to thank God for the people who came into her life as well as for the people who left her life. As a result of her new faith, she forgave everyone she felt hurt her in any way and was now able to live a more fulfilling, satisfied and blessed life.

Acknowledgements

I dedicate this book to all of the exceptional women in my life that pressed their way and laid foundations for many more to come. I could not have done it without God, Reverend Chapman and all my family and friends.

About the Author

Laura Lawson is a first time author who prides herself on having worn the hats of many different women in such a short life span. She is truly a woman of inspiration, a person of true diligence and someone with experience as a daughter, sister, wife, mother and friend to many people in her life. She also has a background in retail management, business, finance, economics, education, consulting and nonprofit management. She believes that through her book _C.P.R for Women_, she will help women make better decisions by showing them how to **C**hoose wisely, **P**repare their mind and **R**eact to life challenges. She believes that there are so many women in need of this life changing message.